SON OF GOD,
SON OF MAN

The 2001 Christian Companion

Son of God, Son of Man
Published by Foundery Press
© Trustees Methodist Church Purposes, 2000

ISBN 1 85852 178 5

Compiled by Susan Hibbins

Printed in Great Britain by Stanley Hunt Limited

CONTENTS

FOREWORD

'Why are you in the religion of the white man?' A question people often ask me. I don't know which white man they have in mind. Is it Jesus they are referring to, since he has so universally been portrayed as a white man? In most stained glass windows Jesus is shown as a white man, and usually with blond hair. It is possible to be in entirely African or Asian congregations and contexts, with all their varieties, and to find that the only white face around is that of the Jesus in portraits and posters on the church walls.

The problem is not the portrayal of Jesus as a white man. Western male artists portrayed Jesus in their own image. This is an attempt to show that Jesus identifies with them. It is reasonable to share these pictures with people throughout the world. The problems come when the white male Jesus is universalised, even though there have been other portrayals of Jesus. As Daleep Mukarji writes in this *Companion*, 'For people like me, born and brought up in the South – the developing world – Jesus was initially someone brought to us along with colonial powers. We saw a western Jesus – blue-eyed, blond and fair-skinned.'

We have no photographs of Jesus, of course. Furthermore, we have different impressions of him from the New Testament writers. Consequently, over the last two thousand years or so, artists (as painters, preachers, story tellers and so on) have proclaimed Jesus according to 'the fashion of their age' and culture. As Doreen Warman writes in the first article of this book, 'It is fortunate for us that we can interpret Jesus to suit every age and clime, for now we can have our own vision of our Lord within our hearts and minds.' The other writers go on to give us their vision from their hearts and minds. Naturally there are numerous visions. Jesus conjures up such images that he is Son of God, Son of Man, Super-Hero, Messiah, Saviour, Entertainer, Artist, Prophet, Liberator, Rabbi, Leader, Healer, Friend, Sinless, Light, Walker, Shield, Vulnerable, Invincible and more, much more. Jesus is such a profound figure that he cannot be totally encapsulated in one image. We must not make the mistake of the past which was to universalise one portrayal of Jesus.

This book does not contain all that can be conveyed about Jesus, nor does it or any writer in it claim so to do. There are numerous other 'visions' from other hearts and minds that are, for example, African, Caribbean, Samoan or Central American. Perhaps this book will encourage some of these other visions to be shared. Readers should explore what is already available. Here is an image I presented in my Address to the Methodist Conference in Huddersfield:

> Indian Dalit theology describes Jesus as the one who identifies with the Dalits, the people who are rejected by society and broken by suffering. The term Dalit comes from 'Dal' which means crushed, broken. It is the name given to broken, split red lentils. It is one of the cheapest forms of food and feeds the poor. Jesus is Dalit.

In the end what matters is that Christians have a life-giving, life-transforming story of Jesus as a special gift to share and live by, without arrogance, in a world of many faiths. It is a story by which to interpret and give meaning to life. We will learn much, and enhance our understanding of Jesus, if we listen to what others have to share, with respect. We need all the help we can get, such as the contributions which follow, to interpret Jesus for our different contexts, to assist us, always, to serve the present age, our calling to fulfil.

Inderjit Bhogal
President of the Methodist Conference, 2000-2001

Son of Man

Doreen Warman

Don't you wish that you had known him? How different life would be if we could travel back in time to Galilee 2000 years ago! If we had actually met this man Jesus – seen his face, met his gaze, at once so penetrating and yet so kind, surely then we would have rushed to sit close to him, to walk by his side or to wash his feet? Hearing his voice, so full of challenge and of truth, surely we would have hung on every word? Nothing would have been too much trouble for us. How could we have uttered a cross word within his hearing or have behaved badly in his sight? We would have followed him to the ends of the earth . . . perhaps. Only it wasn't like that, was it? For even those who were closest to Jesus, his followers and his friends, did not fully understand – or perhaps did not want to hear – the purport of his message.

In the Gospels we read, 'The common people heard him gladly.' They followed him all day, up the hillside, down on to the seashore. They crowded round to listen and to watch his every action – they would not let him go. So what was so compelling about Jesus? We do not know what he looked like. There are no photographs or portraits of him. Artists and painters through the centuries have portrayed the Son of Man after the fashion of their age. The pale, white-robed figure of Victorian art, the black Madonna's child or the Christ of film or musical – Jesus Christ, Superstar – all make some attempt to recreate his image.

It is fortunate for us that we can interpret Jesus to suit every age and clime, for now we can have our own vision of our Lord within our hearts and minds. We recognise him not by his appearance but by his teaching, his acts, his words and his message. His truth is made known to us without the need for visual aids. But how well do we know him? How much do we really listen to him?

Man of Compassion

The crowds who followed Jesus recognised in him a man who answered not only their questions but also their needs. He healed the sick in mind and body, forgave their sins, blessed their children and gave them hope. To the poor, the destitute and the outcasts, who were despised by others, he gave a new sense of worth. Above all he told them they were loved. The people who influence our lives the most are the ones who love us and encourage us to make the most of ourselves. When we invite people to believe in Jesus, we should remember that Jesus first believed in them. This is the Jesus who sees our potential and lifts us up.

Sometimes we behave as though we are pleading with a reluctant God to take pity on us and help us, but in Jesus we see a God who is waiting to do for us far more than we can ask or imagine. This is the Jesus who wept over the city of Jerusalem saying, 'How often I have longed to gather your children together, as a hen gathers her chicks under her wings, but you were not willing,' and 'Do not be afraid, little flock, for your Father has been pleased to give you the kingdom.'

This is the Jesus who condemned the sin but not the sinner: 'Neither do I condemn you; go, and sin no more.' This is the Jesus who uplifted people by raising their self-esteem: 'You are not far from the kingdom.' This is the Jesus who reassured the fearful: 'Do not be afraid.' This is the Jesus who showed tender, loving care.

One of my favourite stories of Jesus is that of Jairus' little daughter whom everyone presumed dead. Mark tells us how Jesus took her by the hand and said to her, 'Talitha cumi!' which means 'Little girl, get up!' Immediately the child got up and he told them to give her something to eat. As a child I spent many months in hospital. Whenever I underwent treatment that was painful or frightening I can remember imagining the hand of Jesus holding mine and comforting me. It never failed! Still today, with all the advances in medicine, it is often the prescription of loving care which brings us through.

The compassion of Jesus painted a new picture of God for all of us – a God of infinite patience and love, sharing with us every experience life can bring.

Man of Challenge

The listening was easy, but then came the hard part, and it is the same for us. For once we recognise the love of God we cannot escape its challenge and our world is turned upside down. To the fisherman his call was 'Leave your nets and follow me'; to the tax collector 'Come along with me' and to all of us, as the writer Eugene Peterson so vividly expresses it: 'Love your enemies – let them bring out the best in you, not the worst. Our Father is kind – you be kind . . . Anyone who intends to come with me has to let me lead. You're not in the driver's seat – I am. Don't run from suffering – embrace it. Follow me and I'll show you how' (Eugene Peterson, *The Message*, Navpress Publishing Group).

It was a message that was too unsettling for most of his listeners. It is a challenge that maybe we today do not wish to hear.

Jesus, a Contemporary Man

Today the words of Jesus are just as relevant, just as compelling as they were 2000 years ago. Every parable, every simile has its parallel in our modern world. The message of Jesus is for all time, and whether we go looking for the one lost sheep on the hillside, or search the Internet for the one piece of information we need, we can still relate that story to our own situation. The griefs and trials which beset God's people then are the ones which face us today. Greed and selfishness continue to pervade our society, and sadness, loss and longing are with us still. More than ever we need to know that God's love will never let us go.

Today I can go round a supermarket with my scanner in my hand, register the barcodes of items I wish to buy and a computer will add it all up for me, provide me with a print-out of exactly what I have purchased and then let me pay by credit card. Then I can wheel my trolley out of the store without having spoken to a soul!

I can press buttons on my phone and receive recorded messages in answer to my questions. Soon I shall not have to move from my armchair in front of the TV screen to order my shopping, pay my bills, bank my money, get medical advice or learn a new language! Information technology has much to offer. But living is about more than learning, and loving cannot be experienced by remote control.

Jesus, the Son of Man, came among us to demonstrate God's love not with a handbook or computer program, not from the platform of a lecture theatre, but by walking our dusty roads, by handling rough pieces of wood, by cooking over an open fire, breaking bread and pouring wine. He touched the lepers and took the children in his arms. He wept tears and suffered pain, ate and drank and laughed, as we do.

God the Creator inspires us with awe and wonder. The vastness and complexity of the universe are beyond our comprehension. We stand on the brink of discovery and are daunted by the prospect of power. But in Jesus, Son of Man, we can recognise a God whose love is always with us, a God in whose hands our future is secure.

'They that have seen me have seen the Father.'

Unto God's will she brought a devout respect,
Profound simplicity of intellect,
And supreme patience. From her mother's knee
Faithful and hopeful; wise in charity;
Strong in grave peace; in pity circumspect.

So held she through her girlhood; as it were
An angel-watered lily that near God
Grows and is quiet. Till, one dawn at home,
She woke in her white bed and had no fear
At all – yet wept till sunshine, and felt awed;
Because the fullness of the time was come.

Dante Gabriel Rossetti

The Incarnation began when Mary said, 'Into thy hands I commend my body'; the Incarnation was 'finished' when her Son said, 'Into thy hands I commend my spirit.'

Warburton Lewis

She is a reed,
straight and simple
growing by a lake
in Nazareth.

A reed that is empty
until the breath of God
fills it with infinite music.

And the breath of the spirit of love
utters the word of God
through an empty reed.

The word of God
is infinite music
in a little reed.

It is the sound of a Virgin's heart
beating in the solitude of adoration.
It is a girl's voice
speaking to an angel,
answering for the whole world.

It is the sound of the heart of Christ,
beating within the Virgin's heart.
It is the pulse of God
timed by the breath of a child.

Caryll Houselander

At the centre of the Christian Gospel is the fact of the Incarnation, the sacramental truth that God was in Christ. He who created a world to show forth his glory, was himself made man. In that flesh we see him who is Spirit and Truth; his voice is the voice that rolls the stars along.

Kenneth Greet

We think that [God] chose this method [the Incarnation] because nothing could have been more effective and persuasive than a deliverance from within. It is a child in a stable, a hand stretched out to heal, a body on a cross, a man miraculously alive again that speaks to our condition. We further think that if in Jesus Christ the divine has entered into the human, then there must be some deep affinity between the two. Although God belongs to the eternal order and human beings are mortal, they are made in God's image. The personal being of humankind echoes however faintly the personal being of God and thus makes way for the possibility that God may unite himself with humankind.

Charles Duthie

By the hand of a child I am led to the throne of the King.

G. W. Russell

The Christian faith makes the astonishing claim that if you want to know the truth about God, you need to look at Jesus. God is like Jesus. So, if faith starts with knowing the truth about God, it starts here – with the knowledge that Jesus has come into the world. The technical name for this is the 'incarnation' and it's what St John is talking about when he says, 'The Word became flesh.' We know that the Son of God has come. My faith is rooted there, with the fact of Jesus Christ.

David Rhymer

Peace is not won
By man's eternal strife,
Peace is not won,
Peace is the power of God
In human life.
He dwells with joy and love,
Is manifest in grace;
The star above his crib,
The light that is his face.

Anonymous

'Thy light is come.' The world had been dark and now all is bright. The world had been empty, then suddenly the whole universe is full; as when in loneliness we hear the song of a bird or see the radiance of the sunset or find ourselves in the presence of the one we love. 'So let the love of Jesus come and set thy soul ablaze.' For God is love and Christ is God.

Allen Birtwhistle

The People's Person

Ray Simpson

Since I have discovered Celtic Christianity Jesus has become more awesome, real and vigorous to me. My blood tingles when I think of Jesus, Son of God and Son of humankind.

I constantly wonder that one of the Three Loves of the eternal Trinity comes bounding down the mountainsides to embrace us on earth. The Nativity is such a great happening that creation itself is affected:

> This night is born Mary Virgin's Son
> This night is born Jesus, Son of the King of Glory
> This night is born to us the root of our joy
> This night gleamed the sun of the mountains high
> This night gleamed sea and shore together
> This night was born Christ the King of greatness . . .
> Glowed to him wood and tree
> Glowed to him mount and sea
> Glowed to him land and plain
> When that his foot was come to earth.
>
> Carmina Gadelica

I constantly wonder that The Infinite One accepts such humbling:

> For nine months he who is angels' Lord
> Was hidden, love's furnace, in a little room
> Humbler than all, whom all adored.
>
> Tadg Gaelach O Suilleabhain

The dignity in this divine humbling is so all-resonating that it changes the values by which we humans live. It motivates me to replace a world of colliding egos with a world of the dignity of humbling. It evokes prayer:

> Babe of Heaven, Defenceless Love
> in order to come to us
> you have to travel far from your home.
> Come to strengthen us
> on our pilgrimage of trust on earth.
> Your birth reveals to us
> the simplicity of the Father's love
> the wonder of being human.
> Help us to live fully human lives for you.

Becoming fully human

Jesus as Son of God is awesome: Jesus as the supreme expression of *Homo sapiens* is galvanising. I think it was Aristotle who pointed out that in order to study any species, you need to choose the best sample of that species. Jesus called himself, according to old translations, 'The Son of Man'. Today we would say he is 'The People's Person'.

What does it mean for us to be fully human, and how does 'The People's Person' help us to become so? These are some answers I have received to the first question: to be real . . . to make good relationships . . . to be a good lover . . . to be sensual, understanding, and beautiful inside . . . to be in touch with your feelings . . . to flow in your potential . . . to have masculine-feminine balance . . . to be healthy in mind and body . . . to be free . . . to be vulnerable . . . to live and die well . . . to appreciate good food, friends, and the wonder of life . . . to be alive with all your senses . . . to be deep but full of fun.

Irenaeus said, 'The glory of God is seen through a human life fully lived.' To be fully human is to tie in with our original intention. To be redeemed is to be redeemed into all that we are meant to be; to be like Jesus. Our humanness is what reflects the likeness of God in us. The image of God in humans is expressed through goodness, through creativity, through moral choice, sensuality, intellect, relationships and worship.

In their first millennia on earth humans spent their energy eking out a living; they had little time to explore the quality of life. Some civilisations transcended that pattern, but this was only for the few who lived on the back of the sweated labour of many. Now, new technology enables us to focus on the quality of life, and the feminisation of society encourages us to explore the inner as well as the outer dimensions of human life.

Churches 'should become the places, par excellence, where the general public can find out how to live fully human lives' (Robert Warren). Jesus is the head of the church, yet second millennium churches often dehumanised more than they rehumanised their members. There were exceptions. The Capella, Padua, for example, symbolises the transition into humanism. Tenderness and the beauty of being human permeate the place. But this humanism was not rooted in the biblical faith of Christianity, and it was soon overlaid and lost sight of. The churches neglected the biblical Wisdom tradition in Christianity, which values the feminine in God and in people. Towers, tasks and tirades were their landmarks. From the churches the people gained a vague impression that God was like a mean boss who tries to find out what people are doing in order to tell them not to. Emerging churches value the feminine in God, and see the church's role as bringing to fullness all that is truly human in each person.

How does Jesus help us to do this? Jesus teaches us how to eat food in the enjoyment of the presence of others. He teaches us the difference between slap-dash and stylish living. He teaches us how to create inner space to love as God loves. He shows us how to distinguish between good and evil by following an inner law that arouses the appropriate emotions. Shame, fear, guilt are signs we are making wrong choices; joy, resolution and confidence are signs we are making right choices. He shows us a way of entering into wonder, a way of being balanced, a way of being present and of being absent.

Vulnerable yet invincible

Jesus models for us how to be vulnerable and yet at the same time, invincible. Church people have been conditioned for centuries to disguise their innermost being. This point is tellingly made in Ronald Ferguson's biography of the Scottish Presbyterian minister George McLeod who, he says, 'was keeping strict controls on access to his innermost core, where the puritan carefully policed the passionate. The language of one's innermost feelings was not in the McLeod family lexicon . . . he had the McLeod reputation of omni-competence to protect and uphold.' (Ronald Ferguson, *George McLeod: Founder of the Iona Community* p.108, William Collins 1990). After a breakdown George had a transforming experience, which enabled him thereafter to model a Christianity which helped people to become more fully human.

The Anglo-Saxon poem, *The Dream of the Rood*, in which the tree to which Jesus was nailed speaks, memorably expresses this noble fusing of vulnerability with invincibility:

> I saw the Lord of humankind
> hasten with such courage to climb upon me . . .
> Then the young warrior, God Almighty,
> stripped himself, firm and unflinching.
> He climbed upon the Cross, brave before many,
> to redeem humankind . . .
> They drove dark nails into me; dire wounds are
> there to see,
> the gaping gashes of malice; I dared not injure
> them.

They insulted us both together; I was drenched
in the blood
that streamed from the Man's side after he set his
spirit free.

To live well, we have to die well. Jesus shows us the way.
A fourteenth-century hermit on the Isle of Farne visualised
Jesus as a latter-day David overcoming one hurdle after
another, the last of which is death:

You are David who scattered with strong arm
your foes
and shattered death's barred gates to free your
own people;
You slew the giant vaunting
and the sons of Jacob taunting
though you had but a sling . . .
Warfare for us waging blithely
to the cross-top leaping lithely
hell's great might you overthrew . . .
Kindest Jesus then uphold us
when death's darkness does enfold us
be our comfort and stay.

The refined molten metal of our forge

Perfect God, perfect human being; two natures, one
Person. Many people cannot reconcile these; they focus on
one and the other becomes distant. Celtic Christians saw
no contradiction here; they perceived Christ as the Bridge
between God and all created life:

O Son of God . . . dear child of Mary, you are the refined
molten metal of our forge.
It is you who makes the sun bright, together with the ice
it is you who creates the rivers and the salmon all along
the river . . .

Though the children of Eve ill-deserve the bird flocks
and the salmon
it was the Immortal One on the cross
who made both salmon and birds.
It is he who makes the flower of the sloes grow through
the surface of the blackthorn
and the nut flower on other trees.
Besides this, what miracle is greater?

Tadhg Og O Huiginn

Given, not lent,
And not withdrawn – once sent,
The Infant of mankind, this One,
Is still the little welcome Son.

New every year,
New born and newly dear,
He comes with tidings and a song,
The ages long, the ages long;

Even as the cold
Keen winter grows not old,
As childhood is so fresh, foreseen,
And spring in the familiar green.

Sudden as sweet
Come the unexpected feet.
All joy is young, and new all art,
And he, too, whom we have by heart.

Alice Meynell

Let us follow the guiding of our star in a childlike spirit, however deep inwards or downwards it may lead us; for we do already realise from afar that peace of mind and larger vision increase, according as we follow this gently attracting, drawing power, and satisfy the demands of this inner guide, and this is irrefutable proof that our spirit is nearing the place of its peace. In this end we find the Child, and in him everything – peace, and poverty of spirit, in the solitude of Bethlehem.

Gerhard Tersteegen

Son of God, Son of Man

Moonless darkness stands between,
Past, O Past, no more be seen!
But the Bethlehem star may lead me
To the sight of him who freed me
From the self that I have been.
Make me pure, Lord: thou art holy;
Make me meek, Lord, thou wert lowly;
Now beginning, and always:
Now begin, on Christmas Day.

Gerard Manley Hopkins

This miracle is enough – that Jesus Christ is God's Word made flesh, dwelling among us. When the wonder of that event really gets hold of me – that Almighty God has taken our nature, really becoming man in order to rescue and redeem us – then I don't find it at all strange that other unique things should have happened that are associated with him.

David H. C. Read

I saw a stable, low and very bare,
*   A little child in a manger.*
The oxen knew him, had him in their care,
*   To men he was a stranger.*
The safety of the world was lying there,
*   And the world's danger.*

Mary Coleridge

> Into this world, this demented inn, in which there is absolutely no room for him at all, Christ has come uninvited. But because he cannot be at home in it, because he is out of place in it, his place is with those others for whom there is no room, with those who are rejected, discredited, denied their status as persons, tortured, bombed and exterminated.
>
> Thomas Merton

If I had known –
Could I know
That they were so important? Just the two,
No servant, just a working sort of man
Leading a donkey, and his wife thereon,
Drooping and pale . . .
There was a sign, they say, a heavenly light
Resplendent, but I had no time for stars.
And there were songs of angels in the air
Out on the hills; but how was I to hear
Amid the thousand clamours of an inn?
Of course, if I had known then who they were –

Anonymous

Still Bethlehem the town
Lies where it lay long years ago,
Still children play through crooked streets
And wander on the hills,
Still men sow seed and harvest grain,
Still women bake.

But all the world
Goes the more bravely to its task,
Because once, long ago,
A little child was born
In Bethlehem.

Anonymous

Blessed be the hour, O Christ, when thou wast born,
and the hour in which thou didst die:
Blessed be the dawn of thy rising again,
and the high day of thine ascending:
O most merciful and mighty Redeemer Christ,
let all times be the time of our presence with thee,
And of thy dwelling in us.

Eric Milner-White

Giving Attention to Jesus

Ian Cundy

'Each of us is unique, yet the story of any one of us is in some measure the story of us all.'[1] I first read those words a number of years ago, but I have come back to them from time to time, because they speak to me at so many levels. They remind me of the amazing variety of the human personality and the fact that among the millions of people in this world there is only one person just like me, and only one 'you'. We are both unique (even if you do have an identical twin!). At the same time they speak of a crucial experience of being human – that we are interconnected. My character and my actions are intimately bound up with the lives and personalities of other people.

One of the joys of a bishop's life is that you meet a rich variety of people. Both in the diocese and through membership of various organisations, I have to be involved with others. Many share my Christian convictions; others belong to different faith communities. Others are agnostic about their faith, some are genuinely atheist. We communicate face to face, by letter, telephone or the Internet. Some of these relationships are of long-standing and have profoundly shaped the person I am – especially relationships within the family – others are more transient, but they still leave their impression on my personality.

But even those that are apparently fleeting can ask searching questions about what it means to be human, from the uninhibited joy of sharing in worship with those suffering from 'learning difficulties' of one kind or another, to the rare privilege of discussion with professors and politicians about the boundaries of knowledge and the shape of our future. The human story, of which you and I are a very small part, is the most fascinating and absorbing story we will ever read, and it is developing in all the wonderful variety of our daily encounters.

But for some of those whom I meet, the connection that I want to make with a man who lived two thousand years ago seems irrelevant, or at best antiquarian. They recognise that our story is in some measure bound up with those of our contemporaries, even with those of our immediate predecessors, but the further you go back in history the less relevance the story seems to have. The dictum of C. S. Lewis that a society which forgets history lives in bondage to its recent past rings few bells for many in the modern world. So why do I go on about a person who lived two thousand years ago? And why do I suggest that if those of us who are privileged to live on the threshold of the third millennium (a dating which is derived from that same historic person!) want to discover what it means to be human, then we should look at the life of Jesus, as well as the network of stories which have shaped us?

One of the parables recorded in the Gospels concerns a group of wicked tenants. The scene was certainly familiar to Jesus and his hearers, but still retains a contemporary ring. A man plants a vineyard, and lets it out to tenants. When his servants arrive to collect the fruit the tenants refuse the landlord's request and treat his servants with hostility and even death. Thinking he is playing his trump card, the landlord sends his son, but the tenants have other ideas: 'This is the heir; come, let us kill him, and the inheritance will be ours.'[2] So what will the owner do? The hearers have no doubt; he will destroy the tenants and give the vineyard to others.

Matthew clearly regarded the parable as told against the religious leaders who had rejected Jesus: 'When the chief priests and the Pharisees heard his parables they realised that he was speaking about them.'[3]   But the story has a message for others as well.

Its impact depends on the assumption that Jesus is talking about God and about himself. God is to be identified with the householder, who created the vineyard in which his hearers are tenants, and Jesus is to be identified with the son. Those who heard it then had no difficulty with the first identification. They believed in God and had little doubt that he had created the world of which we are still the stewards. The religious leaders clearly had difficulty with the second, however, and took precisely the action which the story predicted they would. They could not cope with the claim that Jesus was the son – in that they differed from the tenants – but they destroyed him nonetheless.

In our more sceptical age, we may have to start a stage further back. We are told that the majority of people in this country still believe in God. But have they ever asked themselves: if that is true and God exists, then how might he have chosen to make himself known?   Could the suggestion of the parable not be the best way possible?

In his film *Secrets and Lies*, Michael Leigh creates a plot in which an adopted black woman, 'Hortense', whose adoptive parents have both died, sets out to find her natural mother. The (white) mother, 'Cynthia', has tried to forget her first child, born when she was sixteen, and did not even look at her when she was born. She has no idea she is black ('they got the dates wrong'), even after Hortense has contacted her by phone. The poignancy of their meeting is beautifully played, as incredulity turns to belief and then to mutual recognition and affection. For all their improbability, the two stories are inextricably linked.

Those of us who believe the claim of Jesus' parable can have no cast-iron proof that it is true. There are other possibilities of the way in which God might have communicated with his creation – some contained in the beliefs of other religions. But having been through that same process as Cynthia, from incredulity to recognition and belief, the story of Jesus begins to make sense. If we were God, wouldn't we have chosen this way, above all others, of relating to our creation? And if I allow his story to be in some measure my story, then does it not make sense of my life? To ask those questions allows us to consider the possibility that in the life of this person is a vision of what it means to be human.

Each one of us is unique. As we are approaching ever nearer to the mapping of the human genome, we recognise the complexity of the genetic coding that makes me 'me', and you 'you'. The assertion that there is no one else, nor has there ever been anyone else, just like you and me has acquired a scientific basis, and an improbability beyond all imagining. But we belong together as members of the human race. What it means to be human is a challenge that faces us in our very different context, as it has faced all who have gone before us. There are questions to be faced and opportunities to be grasped in the twenty-first century that our predecessors scarcely dreamed of. We will express our humanity in new ways, but the question remains fundamentally the same.

The quotation with which I began asks us to consider that in some measure the story of anyone I study in history, of everyone I meet in the course of my life, is part of my story as well. This is partly because they too have struggled to find out and to express what it means to be human, and partly because of the interconnectedness that we experience in our daily living. The further we go back in history, the more tenuous we may feel the connections are. But few people are not moved by the words of the Sermon on the Mount, or challenged by the thoughts of Plato, or the wisdom of Solomon – 'as a door turns on its hinges so does a sluggard on his bed' has a contemporary ring!

In the book *This Sunrise of Wonder*, from which the first quotation is taken, Michael Mayne challenges us to restore a readiness and an ability to give proper attention to what is before our eyes, so that, in the words of Augustine, we may 'restore the health of the eyes of the heart by which God may be seen'. For 'if your eye is sound, your whole body will be full of light'. To give proper attention to the person and the insight of Jesus is not irrelevant, not antiquarian, in the twenty-first century. It is rather to recognise that consciously to make his story part of our story is to gain a profound vision of what it means to be human in our context, as it has in every other context for two thousand years.

---

1 Michael Mayne, *This Sunrise of Wonder*, HarperCollins, 1995.
2 Mark 12:7; Matthew 21:38; Luke 20:14.
3 Matthew 21:45.

Do ye remember? . . . Surelye I remember . . .
Were it come April? Were it come September?
Nay friend, nay friend,
It were the latter end
Of one December . . .
We cracked our knuckles at the charcoal ember . . .
Ay, ay, 'twas so,
A many years ago.

Han't ye fergot the Star? . . . I hab't fergotten
Yon Star. Why, wudn't I the first to spot un?. . .
Nay friend, nay friend.
The merricle-star did wend
Sky high, an' brought un'
To some old barton, leaky-roofed an' rotten . . .
Ay, ay, 'twas so,
How many years ago?

Eleanor Farjeon

*We are none of us too poor, or stupid, or lowly –
it was the simple shepherds who saw him first.
We are none of us too great, or learned or rich –
it was the three wise kings who came next and
offered gifts. We are none of us too young, or
too old. There is only one thing against most of
us – we are too proud.*

Michael Fairless

O God,
Let there be a little brightness,
a little warmth radiating from me,
a little epiphany of love and holiness,
        as I kneel
before the birth of Jesus,
grateful for what it tells me of you
and for what it does within me.
Let me be as simple and humble
        as the shepherds,
as wise and worshipping as the wise men,
in the stories of that birth,
and let the Christ child
be born in my heart
to make me with him
        a child of yours,
a brother or sister of him
and so a lover of all
I meet or hear of,
        O Eternal Light,
        O Infinite Love.

George Appleton

O Saviour, we praise you that your coming to earth was not with pomp and ceremony but with simplicity and quietness, that your everlasting Love came to a stable for cattle and a bed of straw. As we look again at the manger of Bethlehem, grant us the wisdom that is revealed only to the childlike heart. Help us to read the goodness of redeeming love in the lowliness of Mary, in the fidelity of Joseph, in the meekness of the shepherds and in the song of the angels upon the starlit hills.

Clement H. Pugsley

The manger where he lay,
New-born upon the hay,
The bench at which he toiled,
The hands his labour soiled,
The simple words he said,
The multitudes he fed,
The grave by which he sighed,
The cross on which he died,
His resurrection face
Bright with celestial grace –
All the long way he trod,
Still speaks the love of God.

Reginald Glanville

One Light remains amid the encircling gloom: the light that lighteth everyone, that flows from the life of Christ, that no disaster can obliterate, that shone on Bethlehem and that not even the darkness of Calvary could extinguish. In the falling twilight it lingers undiminished. 'The light shines on in the dark, and the darkness has never quenched it.'

Frederick Gill

It would be of very little purpose to me to know how God, who is a spirit and not a body, spoke in creating the world. What does matter to me and to you is to know that Jesus, the Eternal Word of God, took flesh and suffered to redeem us.

Catherine of Siena

We have the revealing glimpse of [Jesus] at twelve years old, after which he enters the tunnel of routine only to emerge after many long years. Did the lively spirit never strain at the restrictions? Did he not have to learn like others that ideals and beliefs have to be expressed in real situations from day to day? Like other men, he had a job, family relationships, and the same old view (even if it was a lovely one) outside the window . . . the frustrations of life are real, the discipline of unremitting duty is real, and both can be woven into God's plan, and God's peace. This is no mere pious hope: it is the present experience for Christians, just because God's love in Christ is so thorough and time-taking. He who as a boy was subject to his parents was subject to life's pressures in manhood. In his public ministry, although the routine to some extent would be removed, the frustration and restriction limiting a human life would still be there.

Thomas Baird

I Can See Your Father in You

Susan Howdle

'I can see your father in you': that's a remark frequently made to me, which in my younger years I found both mystifying and irritating. I was puzzled as to what possible resemblance I, as an energetic teenager in the Swinging Sixties, bore to my middle-aged Methodist minister father, and was a bit fed up at not being able to be myself. (My mother was even more irritated, especially when one of her in-laws, quite unintentionally, commented: 'Susan's a lovely child; I can't see a bit of your side in her!')

Now when I'm told I resemble my father, or indeed my mother, I take it as a real compliment. It has also set me thinking about the light it can shed on my Christian experience – although I would want to stress straightaway how much I realise that there will be many readers for whom such family relationships have not been so positive, and who will find other, much more meaningful ways of looking at their life in Christ.

I would have loved to use this space to say something of my father's life and ministry, to show what it taught me about Jesus through the eyes of a disciple. (Not to mention what it taught me about the meaning of ordination, but that's another story!) But to try to recreate the personality of someone whom one holds dear, for the benefit of those who never knew that person, can so often end in frustration for the speaker and for the listener. What was he or she really like? Sometimes we have to accept that our desire to tell, and our desire to know, can simply not be satisfied – in this life anyway.

When I approach the Gospels I sense some of the same frustration, at least for me on the receiving end. Yes, we know that we are not reading biography and that we are on a journey far beyond the quest for the historical Jesus. But what was he really like? Curiosity is still a natural human feeling. Whilst I'm not one who is particularly given to imagining what Jesus looked like, I found myself one day, when listening to Bach's *St Matthew Passion*, speculating as to whether Jesus was a tenor or a bass!

We may wonder about the 'many other things that Jesus did'. Perhaps we long to know them, to settle those fruitless arguments about 'What would Jesus have done?' – or maybe sometimes we'd rather not know! What if we had all those books which the world could not contain (John 21:25)? Or what if there had been the equivalent of a 'fly on the wall' web site, recording every move he made on camera? I believe we would certainly have seen a vivid, challenging person – infinitely more exciting than any of those who offer their dreary doings on the Internet.

Yet to get to the essence of the personality depends not on knowing what they have for breakfast every day, but upon that spark of recognition which lights our imagination and sympathy. So countless millions over the centuries, whether in the church or not, have had their minds and spirits challenged and captivated by 'Western art's most popular character', as my newspaper labelled Jesus in describing the major exhibition at the National Gallery in spring 2000.

But there's so much more to it than that. That exhibition's name, Seeing Salvation, begins to take me to the heart of the matter. It takes me back to the faithful Simeon, inspired by the Spirit to see with his own eyes, in a baby presented in the midst of normal Temple routine by a perhaps somewhat ill-assorted and bemused couple, God's revelation of hope for all people – and back to the 'little old lady' Anna, who went out to gossip that good news.

Why is it good news for me, here and now? Because at the heart of it is an amazing truth: yes, there are indeed very real limits to what we can ever know and understand of the life and death of Jesus, but as we touch even the hem of his garment we can dare to say that we have begun to catch hold of what God is like.

'You can see my Father in me' (remember John 14:9). That's not just a matter – as with me and my father – of a particular smile, or a way of thinking or speaking, but something more than we ever encompass. Jesus is the perfect mirror in humanity of what God is like. The family resemblance is total. I recall those memorable words of Archbishop Michael Ramsey: 'The heart of Christian doctrine is not only that Jesus is divine, but that God is Christlike, and in him is no un-Christlikeness at all.'

Now for me, that certainly does not diminish all the wealth of insights into the nature of God by which our sisters and brothers of other faiths live and which they offer to enrich our own vision of Christ. But what does it mean to me, as a white cradle Christian, to speak of the Christlikeness of God? It means that the very essence of the Godhead is self-giving love. It is a love which is far beyond human thought or language, but the key to it lies in the life, death and resurrection of Jesus. The grace and truth that I need for my life is offered in the glory 'as of a father's only son', seen in one who became flesh and lived and died among us: 'only a suffering God can help' (Dietrich Bonhoeffer).

A few years ago on holiday, while staying in Burgundy, we visited the 'Hôtel Dieu' in Beaune. As Chair of Methodist Homes for the Aged I could almost have claimed the travel costs as legitimate expenses, as I learnt so much about what earlier generations had to teach us about care of the most vulnerable and needy! Here was the re-creation of the medieval hospital where the frailest poor, no longer able to work, were housed, and housed in surroundings that provided comfort and dignity – even, on

Feast Days, with special hangings and bedspreads in fine tapestry. For their inspiration, to grace the altar in that Poor Ward and opened out to its full beauty on Sundays and Feast days, hung the fine large masterpiece by Roger van der Weyden, a polyptych of Christ Enthroned in Glory. But meanwhile, as part of everyday life at the other end of the ward, 'not throned above, remotely high', was a much smaller, life-sized fifteenth century wooden statue of Christ seated, bound and crowned with thorns, silently and agonisingly awaiting his death.

I'm challenged in my own daily life to hold together both these images of Christ, for one without the other can never be the good news of the grace and truth offered to us in him. I was reminded of it when shortly afterwards I read of the fuss created about the painting of the then footballer Eric Cantona, in the form of a revamped version of the famous Piero della Francesca painting of the resurrection of Christ. Christ was sitting triumphant, with Cantona's head superimposed. It was described as a faithful reproduction of the original, apart from, as the press put it, the 'tactful removal' of the marks of the nails in his hands and feet and of the sword in his side. But what on earth – or in heaven – could be less faithful to the original? The victory which gives hope to the world was not won by a Teflon-skinned, invincible superman: 'With one bound he was free.' It was brought about through the man who did not come down from the cross to save himself but stayed there, even in the agony of desolation, so that we, like the Roman centurion, could see his Father in him.

That's the good news for me. But it's also the challenge, in how I then live and, pray God, die. Here I go back to my father, and what he taught me. One of my most prized possessions is a framed 'address' presented to him by a Circuit in which he had served and later been a supernumerary minister, to mark his fifty years as a minister. Of all the many phrases that I treasure, one is very special: 'a dear brother in Christ'. I believe that through his life the people amongst whom he had ministered had been enabled to take hold of the profound truth that, in and through Christ, we ourselves are indeed together God's children. But – to be the children of God? Just think what that could mean. 'I can see your father in you.' 'You're the image of your mother.' Even as I write these words they sound so presumptuous. But remember:

> Beloved, we are God's children now; what we will be has not yet been revealed. What we do know is this: when he is revealed, we will be like him, for we will see him as he is.
>
> 1 John 3:2

And that leaves no room for pride. For the true family likeness, that 'faithful reproduction', will only be seen when the marks of the nail prints are revealed in our lives.

The Jews imagined that they knew all about Jesus – born to Joseph, quite an ordinary child; but Jesus says at one and the same time that he is both the bread that comes down from heaven and a real being of flesh and blood. In later times there were men who were willing to believe in a purely spiritual Saviour but not a flesh and blood Christ. In our own day there are people who unhappily stumble at the same point; but the real mark of the full Christian faith is to believe that Jesus Christ is God made man.

Kenneth Grayston

Jesus was poor and a workman. Astonishing! The Son of God – who, more than anyone else, was free to choose what he would – chose not only a mother and a people, but also a social position. And he wanted to be a wage earner.

That Jesus had *voluntarily* lost himself in an obscure Middle Eastern village; annihilated himself in the daily monotony of thirty years' rough, miserable work; separated himself from the society that 'counts'; and died in total anonymity.

Carlo Carretto

We are told that Jesus grew . . . There was in the background a human home in which there was a family life; there were the hills and the lake, the synagogue, the Sabbath, and the Scriptures. And doubtless also there were occasional visits to Jerusalem at the times of the great Feasts. There was work to be done and the hundred and one things of everyday life. Thirty years is a large part of any man's life, and cannot easily be dismissed in any attempt to understand Jesus . . . it is not without significance that for some years he was working at his trade, labouring as a craftsman with his hands.

W. Lorne Cornish

Jesus was fully human as well as fully divine. He did not take unto himself a vague humanity, but belonged to one race, to one woman. How much she helped him to grow with God's favour resting upon him we can never estimate, but it is significant that the last word from the cross is the first prayer she taught him . . . 'Into thy hands I commit my spirit.' She, through whose trust and obedience he had come into the world, taught her son those same qualities . . . She taught them to him not only in words but also in life, and always he received from her a love that was strong and deep and enduring, so great that it compelled her to come and stand by his cross.

John Dover

Jesus came from God, for God he bore testimony. All his words and works, his desires and dreams hastened on to the time when he could say: 'Go ye into all the world and preach the good news to all nations.' This was the destiny of the good news. It was not an easy task to which Jesus had set his hands and his heart.

J. C. Mantripp

I see him walk among the flowing hills,
Finding God branded on each living thing –
Frail winter sparrows that the sharp air kills,
Spring lilies that out-Solomon a king.

I think he walked beyond the belt of flowers
Into the desert where few strangers trod,
And in those silent, unrecorded hours
Within his own still heart discovered God.

Returning from the desert, love-compelled,
The pulse of mortal living was renewed,
But always, in the largest crowd, he held
Within his heart that God-filled solitude.

Clive Sansom

I wonder what he charged for chairs
At Nazareth.
And did men try to beat him down,
And boast about it in the town –
'I bought it cheap for half a crown
From that mad carpenter.'
And did they promise and not pay,
Put it off to another day,
O did they break his heart that way,
My Lord, the Carpenter?
I wonder did he have bad debts,
And did he know my fears and frets?
The Gospel writer here forgets
To tell about the Carpenter.
But that's just what I want to know.
Ah! Christ in glory, here below,
Men lie and cheat each other so,
It's hard to be a carpenter.

G. A. Studdert-Kennedy

Who is Jesus?

Peter Graves

'If my experience is anything to go by, one thing is certain. As you study theology for the next four years the figure of Jesus will become more and more central to your understanding, your faith and your experience.' The speaker was Dr William Strawson at Handsworth College in 1963. He was addressing our class of first-year students right at the beginning of our course in Systematic Theology. As I look back on those words, I know them to be profoundly true. Indeed, part of the exciting adventure of discipleship is that we never stop discovering more and more about him.

In a Gallup Poll just a few years ago, Americans were asked with which historical figure they would most like to spend a day. Nearly two-thirds chose Jesus and, perhaps most significant of all, thirty-seven per cent of those who did claimed no church allegiance. Why does this man hold such fascination for us?

A brief chapter such as this cannot hope to do more than begin an exploration of his character and significance. I am therefore going to focus on the three images of Jesus that I have found particularly meaningful; after all, as Jesus well knew, the most profound truths are often best expressed in pictures.

1) He brings light in the midst of darkness

Light is one of the most profound and powerful of all religious symbols. In John 8:12 we hear Jesus saying, 'I am the light of the world. Whoever follows me will never walk in darkness but will have the light of life.' It was this text that inspired William Holman Hunt to paint a picture that arguably became the most popular representation of Christ in the English-speaking world. Appropriately housed in St Paul's Cathedral where Hunt is buried, 'The Light of the World' is the third and most well-known painting of the same scene. It is deeply symbolic. Jesus stands knocking at the door of the human heart. Since it is night-time, Jesus holds a lantern. This not only reveals his person, but reminds us that he is the one who himself brings light to the sinner. He knocks on a closed door representing the human mind which can remain obstinately shut. The weeds that surround it represent the neglect and 'sloth' that can all too easily prevent our responding to the light. In the darkness one can see a bat flitting about, a symbol of the ignorance Christ came to dispel. It is also well known that Hunt deliberately did not paint a handle on the outside of the door. As he said himself, 'It is the door of the human heart, and that can only be opened from the inside.' The artist knew that from his own experience for, as he told his friend W. B. Scott, it was whilst he was painting the first version of the picture he was converted to Christianity.

On the first day of the third millennium, on Radio Four, the Prince of Wales broadcast his 'Thought for the Day'. In it he said, 'The likelihood of life beginning by chance is about as great as a hurricane blowing through a scrapyard and assembling a Rolls-Royce.' He talked about life being a 'more profound experience than we are told', and stressed the 'need to rediscover a sense of the sacred in all that surrounds us'. Perhaps the Prince was reflecting on the many signs of spiritual hunger to be found in contemporary society. People are becoming disillusioned with the emptiness of secular materialism. Feeling rootless, lost and alienated, many are confused and perplexed. They wonder about the meaning of life, and long to make sense of reality.

Into such darkness, Jesus brings light. He shows us all we need to know about God, and all we need to discover salvation and make it our own. Furthermore his teaching gives us a framework for living life to the full. He sets out for us where God intends the world to go. He is like the destination to which we look, and towards which we move. In short, he is the light of the world.

2)   He reveals the compassion of God at the heart of the universe

If you visit the Protestant Cathedral in Copenhagen, you can see around its walls a series of statues of the twelve apostles. In the centre, at the high altar, is a magnificent statue of Jesus. In preparation the sculptor, Bertil Thorvaldsen, made a clay model of each of the statues, including the Jesus figure whose arms were held high in a gesture of power, leadership and authority. Having left the clay to harden overnight, he returned the following morning to find that the arms had fallen into a gesture of pleading. At first he was bitterly disappointed, but as he stood gazing, he saw the image of Jesus as the man of compassion. At that moment he became a Christian, and when eventually the statue was finished, he felt led to chisel on its base the words 'Come unto me.'

In this age of tremendous scientific discovery we know more about the universe than ever before. We stand amazed by its vastness and complexity, and marvel at the sense of purpose and design behind it all. As Prince Charles has reminded us, it could not have happened just by accident. It reflects the mind of its Creator. Jesus reveals God the Creator and Father of us all. Everything about him reflects his heart of love and compassion. Thus at the heart of the universe there is not some vast, unfeeling source of energy about which we know hardly anything. Rather there is a God of perfect love who shows us what he is like in Jesus. He assures us that for all our seeming insignificance, we really do matter to him. We are the children he loves so much that Jesus died for us. Now we can experience the reality of a whole new quality of life, the eternal life that reflects the love of Jesus and will never die.

However, this is not just a clue to understanding, or the satisfaction of intellectual curiosity. Really to experience the compassion of Jesus we need to hear and respond to his call, 'Come unto me.' A tourist visiting Copenhagen was intrigued by Thorvaldsen's statue, and wanted to get a good look at the head of Jesus which is inclined and looking down. An attendant came up to him and said, 'If you want to see his face, then kneel at his feet.' We make the love of Jesus our own when in humility we bow before him, then in love and gratitude seek to serve him all our days.

3) He brings hope in the midst of despair

In Auschwitz, a prisoner returned from his daily work assignment to find a group of fellow inmates standing by the barbed wire fence with their heads looking upward. They were looking at a magnificent sunset. The sheer beauty of creation had lifted them out of themselves and transported them into the realm of hope. There was a pregnant silence until one prisoner said, 'Oh, how beautiful the world could be!' The story is told by Dr Viktor Frankl, an Austrian psychiatrist who was himself a prisoner in the Nazi concentration camp. He quotes Nietzsche who said, 'He who has a why to live can deal with almost any how', and then tells how in Auschwitz, as never before, he realised the importance of discovering a sense of meaning and purpose for our existence. Prisoners desperately needed to find something to live for, and then they were able to face the future with confidence and determination.

Jesus is able to pick up the pieces of our broken world, and lead us forward in hope. He offers forgiveness for the sins of the past, and the chance to begin again. He gives purpose and meaning to the present, together with the strength to face the challenge of the unknown tomorrow. He helps us to face the future with confidence, not because we are strong, but because he is with us. He has not let us down in the past, and is ever with us to inspire and enable us to live out the life of victory.

Why, then, is Jesus so central to our Theology, and why do so many still find him so fascinating? Perhaps we should leave the last word to Dr David Jenkins who, when Bishop of Durham, was asked by a television interviewer how he would sum up the Christian message in a nutshell. He replied: 'God is. He is as he is in Jesus. Therefore there is hope!'

[Jesus' baptism] was for him the moment of decision. For thirty years he had stayed in Nazareth. Faithfully he had done the day's work and discharged his duties to his home. For long he must have been conscious that the time for him to go out had come. He must have waited for a sign. For him the emergence of John the Baptist was that sign. This, he saw, was the moment when he had to launch out upon his task . . . he answered the summons and the challenge of God.

William Barclay

Knowing *about* Jesus and *knowing* Jesus is the difference between a second-hand faith and a vital religious experience.

A soldier of World War II

To thee, O Jesus, I direct my eyes;
To thee my hands, to thee my humble knees,
To thee my heart shall offer sacrifice,
To thee my thoughts, who my thoughts only sees;
To thee my self – my self and all I give;
To thee I die; to thee I only live.

Attributed to Sir Walter Raleigh

Fish, chips, mushy peas and two slices of bread and butter

Sue Brecknell

When I say to you the word 'bread', do you immediately think of Jesus? He is probably not the first thing on your mind when you open a new loaf of Mother's Pride with the sole intention of wrapping two slices around several rashers of bacon! Neither would you necessarily think of Jesus when you tuck into a freshly cooked battered haddock, complete with the aroma of vinegar, from the chip shop, unless, of course, it is to say grace.

Jesus, however, was always in the market for a bit of bread and fish.

We are told many times in the Gospels of the eating habits of Jesus, with comment being passed on the suitability of his dinner partners and the things that they got up to during the meal. Luke's account of Jesus' meal with the Pharisees is a good example of this. 'Does he know who this woman is?' thought Simon the host, as a good-for-nothing slapper (or so we are led to believe) starts to take her hair down, wash Jesus' feet and, just for good measure, do a bit of aromatherapy and massage to boot. Obviously, not Simon's kind of dinner guest.

Jesus took bread, gave thanks and gave it to them saying, 'This is my body which is given for you.'

Pat is a feisty Irish woman who is not afraid to speak her mind. When I was introduced to her, she berated me for a full hour about the treatment she had received at the hands of the church. She had been brought up in a convent by nuns and recounted dreadful stories of cruelty and abuse. I sat and listened, unable to make any comment, but feeling each accusation like a sting. Abruptly she changed her tack, telling me of her love of soda-farl bread and her desperate attempts, which had so far failed, to obtain it locally. She told me that she had even taken the bread buyer in Marks & Spencer to task over the issue because they didn't appear to stock it. Still reeling from the ear bashing I had just received, I was very tempted to go down to Marks to see if the chap in question needed therapy!

'People just don't understand,' she said. 'I'm Irish and I need that bread. It's better than sex, fried up for your breakfast.'

Interesting thought!

A week later when I was shopping on the other side of the city, I came across two packets of soda-farl bread sitting on the shelf of the supermarket. They screamed 'PAT' at me so I bought them, made it my business to find out where Pat lived, knocked on the door and presented them to her. She was speechless, just taking the bread and shutting the door. The next time I saw her, she had discovered that not only was I from the church, I was also a member of a religious order. She had also found her voice again. 'You never told me you were a ****** nun!'

Hospitality, or hostility as Terry Wogan describes the practice of giving food and shelter to guests, is something that Jesus practised to perfection throughout his earthly ministry. It was central to his whole purpose of being with others. He said that whenever we give food to the hungry, we are giving food to him. We are in fact living out a Gospel call in offering hospitality to the stranger, and when we do so we are opening up to the mysterious purposes of God. Think for a moment about the disciples on the road to Emmaus. Sad, gloomy, disappointed, thinking and talking about the events of the previous few days. A touch of irritation is shown to the stranger who demands to know what they are talking about: 'Are you the only person in Jerusalem who doesn't watch the news or read the *Sun*? Haven't you any idea what is going on?'

Despite their irritation, they explain the happenings of the previous days and go on to offer him a place to stay and some food as darkness descends. They are perhaps thinking there was something about this man that was interesting but it is not until he breaks bread with them that they realise who this stranger is.

They offer hospitality to the stranger (answering the call of the Gospel), and before you know it, the scene is being set for something astonishing to happen. So amazed are they by this moment of revelation, they immediately walk all the way back from where they have come to tell the other disciples, and those with them, revealing God's purposes to them.

Pat will never forget me – of that I am sure. In many ways, that story is rather like the Emmaus story. We journeyed together, she and I, she talking and I listening. I heard of her pain. I also heard of her pleasure. She talked of her need for bread, and of her bodily needs as a sexual human being. Pat was given bread and, I think, recognised in me something of God that was beyond the pain and beyond the anger she felt toward the church. Can you imagine what was going through her head? Try to imagine the questions she would be asking herself: Why did she do that? I slagged the church off for well over an hour yet she . . . What for? There must be a catch somewhere. She wants me to start going to church . . .

In that one act of sharing bread, Pat was given, I hope, a completely different picture of the church from that which she had experienced before. She had come face to face with Jesus. I too had come face to face with Jesus as I heard her pain. Jesus too had suffered at the hands of the 'church' in his time. Remember the traps laid to catch him out. 'Is it right for us to pay taxes to Caesar?' and the comment 'Can anything good come out of Nazareth?'

The same scenario was awaiting Pat. The question asked of her as a child was, 'What is the catechism?' Now, the place she lives in is always reported as a no-hope estate, and so we could ask the question 'Can anything good come out of Canterbury?'

The passionate bodily experience to which Pat had likened the bread was more accurate and theologically correct than we may care to admit. It is with passion that we remember that when Jesus ate with the disciples for the last time before he died, he took bread and broke it saying, 'Take this bread and eat it. This is my body given for you.'

He did not say, 'Become a member of my club and keep all its rules.'

This is my Body given for you.

At the same meal when Jesus took a cup of wine, he said, 'This is my blood shed for all people.'

He did not say, 'You are not worthy to gather up crumbs from my table.'

This is my blood shed for all people.

After the meal was over, he took water and a towel and began to wash the feet of the disciples. He said, 'I am setting you an example; you should do as I have done for you.'

He did not say, 'Your feet are mucky.'

Do as I have done for you.

And remember, that as well as talking about bread in its literal sense, Jesus said, 'I am the Bread of Life.'

When we turn our minds in the church to mission, how do we respond to the Pats of this world in a way that is authentic and genuine? The Canterburys of this world belong to us. The people living there are part of our family. We all have one Father, our Father in heaven. The Father to whom we pray, 'Give us this day our daily bread. Give us this day Jesus, the Bread of Life who sustains us.' Is our failure to take the notion of hospitality seriously our failure of faith?

How are we to follow the example of Jesus? When was the last time you washed anybody's feet? When was the last time that you shared bread with anyone? When does the penny drop for us as it did for those two disciples on the road to Emmaus? When do we recognise the presence of Jesus, Jesus revealing himself to us in others?

How should the church be involved in sharing bread in its literal sense and its spiritual sense? Have we not seen that sharing in the literal sense with the stranger opens the way for God to work in us and through us, revealing the Gospel message for all?

You may like to know that soda-farl bread is now available in our local Marks & Spencer, and that Jesus still continues to offer hospitality: 'In my Father's house are many mansions. I go to prepare a place for you.'

It is true that, although the Spirit led [Jesus] into the wilderness, no voice had been heard saying, 'Fast for forty days.' But because God had led him into that wild and desolate region, Jesus had to regard all that happened to him there as the revealed will of God for him. He must not take the initiative and lessen his period of testing. He must wait the development of events, wait for God's time when the angels would come and minister to him. Because God was silent for a time, it did not mean that our Lord was God-forsaken.

John Breeden

The sense of being isolated and therefore unequipped is a necessary part, or a necessary stage, of our experience as human beings. It therefore found a place in the life of Jesus: he too did time in the wilderness. And what happened to him there shows us what is happening to ourselves. Here, as always, we see in his life the meaning of our own.

H. A. Williams

When Jesus paid no heed to the devil's suggestion that he should throw himself down from the pinnacle of the Temple, it was because his Father's way of working was the natural way; seedtime and harvest shall not cease. God may work in a mysterious way, but it is a natural way. Much good seed in this wicked world comes, for various reasons, to nothing; but God goes on sowing the seed, and so will Jesus. He will knock at people's doors, though they be too busy to answer. It may mean a Cross, but that is not the last word.

Alex Findlay

Blessed Lord, who was tempted in all things as we are, have mercy on our frailty. Out of weakness give us strength. Grant to us thy fear that we may fear thee only. Support us in time of temptation. Embolden us in time of danger. Help us to do thy work with good courage, and to continue thy faithful soldiers and servants unto our life's end.

Brooke F. Westcott

Christ hath nobody but you to serve him,
No hands but yours,
No feet but yours,
No head but yours,
No heart but yours,
Therefore give him all.

St Teresa

Blest are the ears that hear, the eyes that see,
When God reveals himself in human guise;
Unlearned, little gifted, lightly prized –
Yet they beside the Lake of Galilee,
Saw something that was hidden from the wise,
And seeing, humbly followed after Christ.

Anonymous

A group of fisherfolk . . . They are Galileans, plain men like you and me. But the hour comes when the light has transformed them. From a faltering discipleship they are changed into an apostleship which shakes Jerusalem and with it, the world.

Sydney Walton

The Master said,
 'Come, follow,'
 That was all.
Earth-joy grew dim,
My soul went after him.
I rose and followed,
 That was all.
Who wouldn't follow if
 They heard him call?

Source unknown

He called the unknown best from Peter, James,
And all the rest, who met him face to face,
And lent their lives to his amazing grace
Of humour, irony and insight; flames
Of lambent love in him seared out the shames
Of life-long littleness in them, till base
Was base no more, and even commonplace
Became uncommon, till their names
Grew strong to move a world that would have thought
Them simple, stupid, ordinary men,
As once they had been, helpless for the task –
Till Christ upcaught in them the gold he sought,
Drew forth their deepest selves . . .
Can he again
Do it, if you or I have faith to ask?

Anonymous

When we stop to think about it, recognising ourselves as disciples of Jesus puts everything in our lives into focus. It gives us a measuring stick for making decisions about what we will or will not do. We need to realise that Jesus, too, was a disciple. A disciple is one who learns through association with a master teacher, learns by sharing in the teacher's life as well as listening to his words. Jesus was a disciple of Our Father, and his deepest longing for his own disciples was to bring them into the communion he enjoyed with the God he trusted and in whose love he rejoiced.

Mary Evelyn Jegen SND

Imaginings

Caro Ayres

Jesus and his disciples had been invited to [a] wedding.
(John 2:2)

It was one of those big weddings, you know, where the whole village goes and drinks the place dry. The wine flowed freely, and there was dancing, and jokes, and laughter . . . I didn't know the couple very well, I think they were friends of his mother's, but anyway he was there, so we were all there as well. It was a good time to get to know him a bit better, actually. He was very relaxed, I can tell you. And then the wine ran out. Bit embarrassing, really, for the family – but what can you do? The word went round, and gradually people got a bit quieter, and a bit more subdued. Until it got to his mother, of course. 'Jesus,' she says, 'they've run out of wine.' The look on his face – sort of puzzled, almost disturbed, a gentle disquiet. But the look on hers – expectant, anticipating, waiting in confidence. She'd already told the servants what to expect. There was no doubt in her mind at all as to what was going to happen.

Well, the rest is legendary. It was the talk of Galilee for weeks – and it took us weeks to shake off the reputation. 'Mine's a large one, Jesus!' they would cry. It all happened so quickly after that. It was as if – as if she had opened the floodgates, released something, set it off. Her confidence in him was complete, and now he had fulfilled her expectations, it was time to move on. He was ready.

So when the Samaritans came to him, they urged him to stay with them, and he stayed two days. (John 4: 40-41)

I was number three. There were two before me, and two, maybe three, after me. I don't know what happened, fault on both sides, I suppose, people change. And she did change! No, not during our marriage but after, when she met that Jewish preacher. Funniest thing, you know, she said he told her everything she ever did. Imagine that – someone like him even knowing, let alone caring about a Samaritan! Of course we all piled out of town, to see this for ourselves. He spoke to us – he didn't stop until sundown. The time just flew by!

By then it was far too late to be going anywhere. But how could we ask him into our village? That sort just weren't interested, normally. So imagine our surprise when not only did he say yes, but he came for two whole days! The whole village got involved, and we all came to believe what he said. How could you not? Yes, we had the Saviour of the world, the real Messiah, to stay in our place. He just came, and sat and ate and talked and played with our children – as if he was one of us! You've got to understand – this just didn't ever happen! It was the first time ever! And we all said, 'Let it be like this from now on. Let us be like him. Forget division and doctrine and rules and jumping through hoops – let us be like him.'

There is a boy here who has five small barley loaves and two fish. (John 6:9)

He was always giving things away. The previous day, he'd given his sandals to this beggar. I ask you! We barely had enough food for ourselves. Generous to a fault, he was – I mean, who else would offer the smallest packed lunch you've ever seen to a crowd of five thousand people? But we were hungry – yes, I was there as well. The whole world was! It was heaving, hot, and of course the crowd wasn't exactly well-endowed – he didn't seem to attract people who were. So by mid-afternoon we were ravenous.

That's when I saw the boy go up to one of the helpers, holding out his lunch. I could have died of embarrassment! This lunch is going straight back, I thought – how could that possibly help? But Andrew simply offered it to Jesus. Well, now the fur is really going to fly, I thought! But Jesus just accepted it. I couldn't see what happened next, but before long we were wolfing down the food, and he carried on, right round the hill, giving it out until everyone had had enough. And I mean enough – we ate and ate until we were full. I don't know how he did it, but I do know he turned that small, worthless offering into something that satisfied us. Something about him obviously impressed the boy – I haven't seen him since that day. I think he decided to follow the preacher.

Woman, where are they? Has no one condemned you?
(John 8:10)

I was one of the first to realise what he was saying. Suddenly it clicked. He really had us this time! We spent ages trying to trap him, but we never once got him. He always managed to turn the tables on us, and usually made us realise that we were the ones with the problem. Like with this woman – to us it was an open and shut case. She was a whore. She had been caught red-handed. She deserved to be punished, and the punishment was laid down in the law. We had him! But, as ever, it was the other way round. What he said – it was a judgement on us, on our morality, our way of doing things, not her's. In his mind, she was no different to the rest of us – no one's perfect, are they? He made no distinction.

So I was one of the first to go. It took some of the youngsters a bit longer, but I knew what he meant straightaway. I didn't go away; I hid behind a pillar, because I wanted to see the real Jesus, to see what he did when no one else was around. And again, he confounded all expectation. He didn't even tell her off, and he certainly didn't condemn her. He just told her to go back to her life, and not to sin any more. Just like that. It simply can't go on. We'll all be out of a job if we let this continue.

When Jesus saw her weeping, he was greatly disturbed in spirit and deeply moved . . . Jesus began to weep. (John 11:33, 35)

I like a good funeral, me. Lazarus – now his was a grand send-off. I knew them all well, especially Mary. She'd changed, you know, ever since she met that Jesus . . . So when Lazarus got sick, she asked him to come because she knew he could help. She waited for days, and he didn't come. Then Lazarus died. She was devastated. I mean, it's bad enough that your one and only brother has gone, but to be let down in such a way by a friend! We tried to help her, to make her feel better. To no avail. She didn't go out to see him when he did come. I think it just hurt too much, knowing what a difference he could have made. But when he called her, she went. There was no anger when she reached him, she simply said, 'He wouldn't have died if you'd been here.' And burst into tears.

And this really got to him. You could see it in his face. He felt her pain – not only at losing Lazarus, but also at the way she felt he had let her down. So he began to cry, with her, in front of everyone. And then we knew that he had come because he loved Lazarus, and Mary, and Martha. After that, of course, the miracle happened. Lazarus lived to tell the tale. And me, well, I felt it was time to stop going to all these funerals, and start enjoying life.

Jesus calls his would-be disciples to take the risk of putting their faith in the unseen kingdom whose presence he proclaims and embodies, rather than in the visible realities of a world doomed to destruction; he calls us to live in the conviction that, hidden behind the world's imperfections, there is a trustworthiness which finally will not let us down. And Jesus, too, puts himself at risk in an imperfect world – a world which crucifies him. Thus does God work, by turning to his own ends those things which appear to conflict with his purposes, and he calls his people to the 'risky' business of losing life in order to find it.

Brian Jenner

Here, Lord, is my life. I place it on the altar today. Use it as you will.

Albert Schweitzer

Christ to me has always been the peerless Knight and Leader at all times. What Christ seems to be asking me is: 'Have you the courage to follow me?' 'Follow me and I will make you fishers of men' has been on the wheel of my ships for the last forty years, and that is increasingly my theology.

Wilfred Grenfell (of Labrador)

Remember, that whatever may be said, there is no one who will say that if you open the door to Christ and let him into your life, you will make a mistake. No one can ever say that the entrance to this Friend would do other than elevate your whole existence. To multitudes it has been the one joy and strength of frustrated and broken years. Let Christ in.

Robertson Nicoll

Being a Christian in a general kind of way must be changed to discipleship of the man of Nazareth. We must set ourselves to learn the great truths he taught; we must be ready to make him the Lord and Master of our lives; we must follow him wherever he leads us. If anybody thinks this is easy, it is because he does not know the message of the Gospel or the meaning of true discipleship.

Kenneth E. Roach

The follower of Jesus is a labourer, but he is a labourer together with God. He is the man with a hoe, but he has his part in the harvest whose reapers are the angels.

F. C. Peabody

Jesus set out with a small group of sympathisers, stopping wherever he could get a hearing. Living frugally and treated to all sorts of different responses by people who, depending on what they were looking for, saw in him so many contrasting things, he quickly became one of the 'odd' people who by the activity in which they are engaged force people to ask questions of themselves. Here again he was 'free', released from the everyday ties of the world, leaving home, work and family, leaving the dead to bury their dead, taking the natural world of lilies, fields, foxes and birds as the model for life. In this way he met the people – especially those whom a rigid and stressful society had also, without choice, made into misfits.

Bryan Rippin

Who answers Christ's insistent call
Must give himself, his life, his all,
Without one backward look.
Who sets his hand upon the plough,
And glances back with anxious brow,
His calling hath mistook.
Christ claims him, wholly for his own;
He must be Christ's, and Christ's alone.

John Oxenham

The source of all our freedom is the freedom of Jesus Christ. By our association with him we are invited into the kingdom of liberation and love. We pledge our faith, 'green as a leaf'. We receive the spirit that disentangles us from sin, from the narrow perspectives of the law, and from the fetters of fear. We join all of creation in struggling to reject what is evil, in submitting to the greater law of love, and in sharing in the glorious freedom of those who belong to God.

Joan Puls

It was through constant prayerful contact with the Father that Jesus received the grace and the power to work miracles and alleviate suffering. The same must be true of us, his followers today, who seek to serve him in whatever field, including that of social concern.

Michael Palmer

It is not sufficient to take our religion from what we read or the sermons we hear preached. We must drink from the fountain-head of life. We must live in constant fellowship with Christ who, as he comes into our lives, will increase our experience of life, which is life indeed.

C. Edgar Wilkinson

The Nothingness of the Son of Man

Julie M. Hulme

Reb Azriel visited the seer of Lublin.[1] Reb Azriel was puzzled. He believed he was wiser, more knowledgeable and more learned than the seer, so why was it that pupils flocked to the other to learn the ways of God, and not to him? The holy man replied that he didn't understand it either, then added, 'But perhaps this is the answer: you don't understand why the people don't come to you, and so they don't come to you. I don't understand why they come to me, and so they come to me.'

I confess to having more than a little sympathy for Reb Azriel, as humility has never been one of my strong points, either. Humility is the inward readiness to place oneself wholly at the disposal of another. It is a tendency and an ability for which we may be gifted, but which can also be learned, willed. For if we are literally 'full of ourselves' – full with an awareness of ourselves – then there is little space left for the other. Which is why pride is an obstacle to compassion, and the route to humility lies through poverty of spirit, where our only awareness is of how much we need God if we are to pray, love, endure.

There are false forms of lowliness: in *David Copperfield* by Charles Dickens, Uriah Heep adopts humility as a means of serving his own corrupt ambitions. Similar to this is the 'humility' where we ensure that everyone is aware of our self-denial, as in the case of the woman of whom it was

---

1   *A Thread of God: Journeys towards Reconciliation*, Albert H. Friedlander, SCM/Trinity Press, 1990 p.5

said that, 'She is always sacrificing herself for others – and you can tell who they are by their haunted expressions.'

Many people, especially many women, retain a low self-image which is an inaccurate assessment of their abilities, but which they prefer not to change because it is more comfortable to think meanly of themselves than to take on the responsibilities of personal power. Here, 'humility' is a means of evading the truth – and its demands.

Again, it is often assumed that to be humble is to be brought low by circumstances or suffering, but this too is false, because such degradation is contrary to God's intention and generally destructive. Indeed, the way of distinguishing between true humility and its many false forms is by asking: 'Is this creative? Does it speak of transforming love?'

My own problems with humility go back to my adolescence when a surfeit of criticism persistently belittled my three cherished dreams of continuing my education, becoming a writer and dedicating my abilities to God. I compensated by becoming armoured in self-belief and unwilling to accept any advice, while inwardly I was desperate to be received unconditionally, whether I believed in myself or not.

Amazingly, wonderfully, my three dreams have been fulfilled. Now in my early forties, I am blessed by self-fulfilment. And yet I have brought myself with me – that demanding self who fills my awareness with my complaints, concerns and feelings, my interior monologue, my posturing before the world. And I am challenged by one who never thought in terms of self at all. Or if he did, knew how to set his own needs aside so as to be completely at the disposal of the other.

It seems as though Jesus was able to do this – not occasionally, but constantly – without any resentment, let alone any complaint. Or was it that he had also learned how to contain, surrender and transfigure the outraged feelings that persistent loving stirs in us as the self is denied again and again and again?

The humility of Christ is at the core of his humanity – and his sinlessness. Whatever it means to say that Jesus was without sin, it surely means that he was humble, that he was other-centred, that his compassion and generosity placed him at the disposal of those who needed him, and that this was not a show of availability, but the complete gift of the heart. In describing the attitude of Jesus towards God, and towards those around him, we may wish to use words like self-denial, self-surrender, self-submission. But even to speak like this is to put too much emphasis on the self. And it raises the question: did Jesus have any awareness of himself at all?

Again and again in my relationship with this man, I am stumped by his apparent lack of self-regard, his refusal to claim anything for himself, his preference for hiddenness, his insistence that he is a pointer to God and not the hero others yearn for him to be. We claim, in faith, that Jesus Christ was the Son of God. Saviour. Messiah. We imagine him in the role we would have him play. The super-hero. The man of power. The healer-teacher-exorcist with a miracle for every ill and an answer for every accusation. The one who will vindicate us, beat back our enemies, establish our values, give us back the land. There are stories and texts which can be used to defend such interpretations, but the key question remains: Who does Jesus think he is? Or rather: Does he think of himself at all?

The title he seems to have preferred was Son of Man. Man. The human instrument of God's judgement on earth.[2] But

---

2 Daniel 7:9-14. The promise of worldly authority in verse 14 was experienced by Jesus as a temptation which he set aside (Matthew 4:7-10; Luke 4:5-8).

how does he understand his mission? His recorded activity suggests a human being who allows himself to be a space of encounter between God and the next needy person who crosses his path. And it may be that the clearest clues to his inner world are not in the statements he made about his work, or in the assertions others made on his behalf, but in the way he taught his disciples to live, and a recognition of what this spiritual dynamic does to a human being. Read his teaching, attempt living it, and while doing so, reflect on what it does to the soul.

If Jesus Christ was truly holy and humble, he himself would have been the last one to know it. For him, too, the road to humility lay through poverty of spirit, knowing his need of God. Which suggests that, despite being filled with the Spirit at his baptism and affirmed by the experience of the Transfiguration, for most of the time his inner life was a desert. It suggests that the Temptation was not a single episode, but that throughout his ministry he carried the wilderness within his heart. It suggests that when he reached out his hand to heal or cleanse, feed or bless, he knew what he had to do and what God was capable of doing, but he did not know that it would happen, once again, at his asking.

We tend to ignore or deny the depth of Christ's humility precisely because it demands of us what we least want to offer – ourselves – and because we do not see with any clarity how such spiritual poverty can make sufficient difference to the difficulties we face. So instead we hold out for a hero, someone who will solve our problems, meet our needs and not ask too many questions about what our desires might be. In this sense, the charismatic Christ is not so different from the Messiah that the disciples wanted to see in Jesus. Even when he is being a Servant King, he is still given capital letters. He is still in command of the situation – the one thing a genuine servant is not.

It may be that we have been misled by the deference of John the Baptist, the faith of the first evangelists and the noise of our own spiritual ambition to misunderstand what Jesus is telling us about the redemptive humility of God. Perhaps when Jesus says that he and the Father are one, he is not speaking of a blessed communion with the divine, still less a status given or attained, but the extent to which he himself had been wiped out by grace. Perhaps Jesus' deepest awareness was of God who withdraws so as to give us room to grow; who remains hidden so that we must interrogate the echoes of our emptiness; who moves on so that we can never settle down. Perhaps for Jesus 'Abba' was as much ache as intimacy.

Even the 'I am' sayings in John's Gospel may not be statements of identity as much as different ways of saying 'I am nothing.' The light by which you read, the door through which you pass, the road on which you walk. The shepherd you rely on but take for granted, the bread that is poorest, most basic food, the life you are scarcely aware of possessing. In other words, a transparency, a means to an end, a space of encounter. 'Why do you ask me who I am? What does it matter? Look at God. Serve the other. In all things, love.'

I believe Jesus of Nazareth fulfils our deepest human hopes and clarifies our deepest human fears, but somewhat strangely. For he takes our hopes far beyond what most of us consider realistic, telling us that we can live forever with God; and he brings our fears into an almost punishing light, telling us that we can utterly ruin ourselves and our world by loving badly.

Thus Jesus' life makes our lives dramatic. Like a story that soon will reach its climax, our time grows tense when we stretch it on Jesus' frame. The more intimately we know Jesus' life, the more it tunes our significance, our lives, into a reflection of his death and resurrection. What are we dying for, what are we choosing against? What will we rise to, how shall our last numbers tally? When Jesus burst upon the Israelite scene, he laid down this most forceful challenge: 'The time is fulfilled, and the kingdom of God is at hand; repent, and believe in the Gospel' (Mark 1:14). I believe he continues to lay down this most forceful challenge wherever we allow him on to our scene.

So for me, the motive of the Christian faith, its cause and source, is the power or allure of Jesus himself.

John Carmody

For the strength of his body, and the firmness of his tread,
For the beauty of his spirit, and the laughter in his eyes,
For the courage of his heart, and the greatness of his deeds,
For the depth of his love, and the people it makes anew,
For the strength of his friendship when we dare to trust his love,
For the knowledge of his presence at each turn of the road,
  We thank you, Lord.

Godfrey S. Pain

The simplest sights he met,
The sower flinging seed on loam and rock;
The darnel in the wheat; the mustard tree
That hath its seed so little, and its boughs
Wide-spreading; and the wandering sheep; the nets
Shot in the wimpled waters – drawing forth
Great fish and small – and a hundred such
Seen by us daily, yet never seen aright,
Were pictures for him from the book of Life,
Teaching by parable.

Edwin Arnold

When Jesus talked about the kingdom, it was not a matter of advising people to stand still and simply not to do certain things . . . for him this kingdom was an adventure; it was not for people who thought they had arrived; it was for those who could share in its growing power. Hence he challenged one man to sell all he had and give it to the poor; another to gamble everything he owned in order to win the pearl of great price; and eleven reluctant disciples to go out into a tottering world with nothing to support them except the promise of his presence.

Donald MacLeod

And him evermore I behold
Walking in Galilee,
Through the cornfields' waving gold,
In hamlet and wood and in wold,
By the shores of the beautiful sea.
He touches the sightless eyes;
Before him the demons flee:
To the dead he says, 'Arise':
To the living: 'Follow me!'
And that voice still soundeth on
From the centuries that are gone
To the centuries that shall be.

Anonymous

It is conspicuously evident that the salvation of individual souls was [Jesus'] supreme concern . . . Parables, miracles and teaching all converge on this one aim, and reveal his special interest in the individual as the object of his appeals, his solicitude and his Gospel. He was the real initiator of spiritual autonomy for the individual, and he called his followers to share his personal communion with his heavenly Father.

Sydney G. Dimond

He spoke of grass and wind and rain,
And fig trees and fine weather;
And made it his delight to bring
Heaven and earth together.

He spoke of lilies, corn and vines,
The sparrow and the raven;
And words so natural, yet so wise
Were on men's hearts engraven.

T. T. Lynch

The connection between love and life is fully indicated in the life of Jesus Christ. He illustrated, rather than defined, love by illuminating at all points the meaning of life . . . He dismissed nothing from his heart that expressed the beautiful, the good, and the true. Birds, beasts, waves of the sea, masses of mountains, the colour of the bazaar, the skill of the craftsman, the patience of the farmer – these were all taken into his hospitable heart.

J. Henry Bodgener

The Art of Christ

Phil Summers

The great thing about the accounts of Jesus' life for me is that he is an entertainer. He draws the crowds and keeps them. He knows how to communicate. It seems to me that people hang on his every word. They follow him to see what he will do next, how he uses the world around him to share with them his vision of the kingdom. Jesus has so many ways of communicating. The traditional methods are available to him, such as reading and commenting on the Holy Scriptures, or sharing stories with all who would listen. But Jesus goes beyond the use of words as he dramatises his message with actions.

Jesus uses the finest of dramatic pauses when he crouches down to draw in the sand as people wait to hear his views on what should be done with the woman caught in adultery. He quickly converts the disturbance and shock of a man being lowered through a roof into a concentrated, if tense, word to the teachers of the law. He takes hold of life around him, either literally, when he places a small child in front of his followers or when he points out the different people offering their gifts at the Temple. He knows he has the full attention of a whole town when he stops and causes all to look up at a small tax collector in a tree. He is sure of the indignation that will grasp people's imagination when he shares a meal within the sinner's own home. And then there are the grand theatrical moments that Jesus produces so well, none more so than his entry into Jerusalem, riding on the back of a donkey like a victorious king. Jesus presents himself well; he is a fine artist. On that final Thursday night before his arrest he takes the simple things on the supper table and fills them with symbolic meaning. He gives to his disciples, and to us, a most powerful picture of a broken body and a chilling image of blood being spilt.

As an artist myself, both dramatic and visual, I am drawn to the way Jesus communicates. This came home to me most clearly when I worked together with a group of artists in preparation for a young people's summer school. The project is known as 'Kick Up the Arts' and is supported by the Methodist Church under the umbrella of the Methodist Association of Youth Clubs. Each summer over four days, young people between the ages of thirteen and twenty-five gather to share in various art workshops. From up and down the country young actors, dancers, musicians, photographers, video makers, singers and artists of all kinds gather to develop and share their skills.

The tutors for 'Kick Up the Arts' are all volunteers, some professional teachers in their own right and others gifted amateurs. While we were considering future plans we were asked to explore the way we worked with our young artists. What were the values and the purposes of developing creative arts with young people? As tutors from different fields of art, as well as different Christian denominations, we started to 'brainstorm' our ideas. We eventually came up with two lists, one for values and one for purposes.

As values in the development of art with young people we suggested this list:

- Integrity
- Honesty
- Aware of the power of art
- Courage
- Effort
- Love of self and others
- Inclusiveness

These were the things that we hoped young people could bring to their work and the values that we, as tutors, could encourage them to develop. Integrity and honesty are important when anyone approaches their art. It can lead to the best work being produced, as there are no limits created by mistrust of either the creative process or the artist. We are aware how strongly differing forms of art can affect individuals. This is true of the artist and of those to whom the art is presented. Young artists need to be aware of their own abilities to produce and control 'powerful' art. Courage is in the list because, when one is being honest, it is possible to reveal a great deal of yourself through the artistic process. This self-revelation can, for many, take a great deal of strength and risk taking. Our course is presented in a Christian context and so we felt that it was important to understand that whatever is being communicated through our work Christ's loving principles are held in place. Again, inclusiveness is a value that springs from our Christianity. Art can be used to exclude and, as a result, can be damaging. The artist must strive towards work that can, at least, be approached by all.

The list of the purposes of art went like this:

- To express feeling
- Has meaning
- To be explorative
- To provoke a response
- For self-awareness
- To fulfil the need to be taught how to see/listen
- To be disturbing
- To be dangerous
- For communication – team building
                      – community

As a group of artists putting ideas together, we realised that the subject was more involved. I don't have the space here to go into great detail, but it is clear that art fulfils many purposes. A way of expressing things, a way of communicating meaning, a way of exploring concepts and ideas: all of these things are ways in which art helps us as human beings. In our conversations we touched upon the more controversial purposes of art. Art in all its varying forms can be disturbing, it can be upsetting. Through art we can experience thoughts and emotions that we would rather not deal with; it can touch us at a level that makes us feel uncomfortable. But the exploration of self through art can also be positive. We may not always be comfortable with the process, but the self-awareness to which it leads can be of great benefit. Through art we can experience the world in new ways, and we can see or hear that which surrounds us in new ways. Our understanding of life and the way we live it can be enhanced. Art can communicate ideas from the artist to those who receive the art, or it can enable people to communicate with each other through their joint experiences of the art. Small groups are enabled to come together at a deeper level of understanding, or larger communities are enhanced by the art they are involved in.

It was at this point that the name of Jesus came into the conversation. As we looked at our lists, outlining our values and purposes, someone pointed out that they could be lists of how Jesus approached his ministry, Jesus' own values in the communication of his message of the kingdom of God being at hand. In the way that Jesus deals with people there is a strong integrity in his various methods of communication. The way he works is never for his own glory but for the glory of his Father. He is tremendously aware of the power of his communication skills and deals with differing situations according to their need. He is happy to be forthright and dramatic with those of great power; witness the way he almost arrogantly refers to the rocks and stones crying out 'Hosanna' in response to the temple priests' call for silence. He is equally at home using a more gentle approach, though no less direct, when circumstances require it, as when he talks to the Samaritan woman at the well. Much of what Jesus does is confrontational and that takes effort and courage. His love for others, and indeed of self, is clear.

What were Jesus' purposes? Look again at the 'purposes' list for approaching art. Again there are great similarities. Jesus expresses both feeling and meaning, whether it is anger at the suffering caused by a skin disease, or his explanation of God's willingness to forgive. He encourages the rich young man to explore meaning in his life, he provokes a response from followers and enemies alike. He is fully aware of his role in the world as he explains to his disciples how 'the Son of Man must suffer'. In his presence people learn to see in a new way, they are disturbed out of their old ways of prostitution and corruption. He builds a team around him and inspires whole communities to hope. His crucifixion shows us how dangerous his communication with the world was.

The supreme communicator, that is Jesus, is an inspiration. To me Jesus is an artist, and as an artist working as a minister I find that his example, in approach and practice, is invaluable.

I marked too that when he came among us, ordinary things seemed noteworthy and common events had more of a rarity. The field flowers were more beautiful, and the sky of a deeper blue when he was near. Life, when we saw it through his eyes, was full of divinity, and held nothing meaningless or dull. The teaching was to me greater by far than the healings, for I felt that it freed people from burdens heavier than all their diseases. The Jewish religion laid a heavy yoke upon people. But the teaching of Jesus freed my mind. When he talked of God, no rebellion was possible, for he spoke of what he knew. He did not teach as the Rabbis did, as if the mystery of the knowledge of God was too great for an ignorant man to understand, nor did he talk of the care and ceremony with which God had to be approached. He spoke as if all people might know God if they had but the will. When he talked of God's love for people, and of what God asked of people, I felt he told us of what he himself had learnt, and of what I, too, could learn. It seemed that even the most simple could understand.

From *By An Unknown Disciple*

May we be found of him who came to seek and to save that which was lost, and be numbered among his own. May the Good Shepherd lead us day by day. When he calls his own by name, may we know his voice, and follow him.

A. Morris Stewart

What was his creed?
I do not know his creed, I only know
That here below he walked the common road,
And lifted many a load. He was for ever bold
To stand alone to face the challenge of each day,
And live the truth.

H. N. Fifer

Jesus rubbed shoulders with self-righteous religious leaders and political despots; with people who had divided loyalties; with tyrants, exhibitionists and fools. He sought to show them that material needs, political interests and organised religion were so much less important than the spiritual truth soundly established in human hearts. That is exactly why he committed himself unreservedly to the task of revealing God.

William B. Taylor

He noticed! That was characteristic of him; wherever he went his alert eye took in all that was happening. There are people who move in and out among their neighbours wearing blinkers; there is a great deal they fail to notice. They are detached and unobservant because they are self-absorbed. It was never so with Jesus. He entered into the lives of people. He put himself in their place, saw with their eyes, felt what they were feeling. Intuitively, he realised their problems, sensed their needs, reached out to them a helping hand.

Robert J. McCracken

As a mother stills her child,
Thou canst hush the ocean wild;
Boisterous waves obey thy will
When thou sayest to them, 'Be still.'
Wondrous Sovereign of the sea,
Jesus, Saviour, pilot me.

Edward Hopper

We know from the Gospels how Jesus captivated people who came into his company. Though he was a carpenter, the disciples knew that he was Master when their boat was caught in a storm on the lake. A paralysed man carried on a mattress knew that Jesus could pardon his sin. An outcast leper knew that Jesus could make him clean. In Jerusalem, when Peter and John bravely faced the authorities after they had healed a lame man, 'they took knowledge of them that they had been with Jesus'.

Anonymous

I remember one evening I stood on the shore of Galilee, and watched the fishermen bringing in their boat. The years roll back, and I see Jesus, not always asleep in the boat but sometimes straining at a rope or taking an oar, making the last few miles easier for tired men . . . My finite mind cannot comprehend the mystery of the Eternal, but I can see Jesus and begin to know God. So for me his love is no mere abstraction. It gives me a hand with the ropes, and is with me in the storm, and, I trust, will help me bring my little ship safe into harbour.

Leslie F. Church

Grant that the remembrance of the blessèd Life that once was lived out on this common earth under these ordinary skies may remain with me in all the tasks and duties of this day. Let me remember:

His eagerness, not to be ministered unto, but to minister
His sympathy with suffering of every kind
His meekness of bearing, so that, when reviled,
    he reviled not again
His steadiness of purpose in keeping to his
    appointed task
His simplicity
His self-discipline
His serenity of spirit
His complete reliance upon his heavenly Father in
    heaven

And in each of these ways give me grace to follow in his footsteps.

John Baillie

[Jesus] spoiled none of his gifts by haste, could wait as well as work, did nothing before the time, rose early to pray, gave nights to communion with God and found leisure to talk with a woman by the well and watch the children at play. He knew how to be alone, but he was not a recluse. The Man of Sorrows and not less the Man of Joys: serious but not strained, his humour without levity, utterly kind and utterly inexorable, tolerant and uncompromising, full of grace and truth.

Russell Maltby

Yet without Sin

John Austin Baker

He was sinless. So we who are Christians have been taught from our first days in the faith, as all Christians before us were. 'He knew no sin,' writes Paul. 'He committed no sin,' writes Peter. 'Not a High Priest unable to sympathise with our weaknesses,' testifies Hebrews, 'but one in every respect tested as we are, yet without sin.'

It must be so, for we have God's assurance on the matter. Were it not so, would God have raised him, uniquely of all humankind, from the dead? The argument seems unanswerable – but what do we mean by it? What is it, to be sinless? The question touches us nearly, for one of the gifts the Spirit seeks to create in us, eventually at any rate, is freedom from bondage to sin. What is it we are meant to become? Or can we never know till we are there? And if not, how can we know what we mean when we say that Jesus was sinless?

One point we need to get clear. Sometimes Christians say, 'Of course Jesus was sinless – he was God, wasn't he?' Now it is true that God is sinless, but that is because he can't sin. He is in himself complete and perfect goodness. So it's no compliment to God to say he is sinless. He can't help it. But Jesus wasn't just God. He was God living a genuine human life as one of us, and that means he could have sinned, because real human beings can always sin. But Jesus, we believe, did not.

Nevertheless, outside the churches, there are plenty of people who dismiss this claim as plainly false. And can even we, as Christian believers, honestly say that none of the stories in the Gospels gives us a moment's disquiet on this count? Those of us who are called to preach, have we never made heavy weather of young Jesus staying behind in Jerusalem without a word to anyone or, later, of his violence in the Temple? Then what of his dismissive harshness to his mother at Cana, his cursing of the fig tree, his savage language about the Pharisees, his allusion to Gentiles as 'dogs' when approached by the Syrian mother anxious for her daughter? In this Christian generation, too, are we not less complacent than our forbears about his insistence on the torments of hell for the unrepentant wicked?

All these things, we may fairly say when challenged, can be explained or put in a different light. We can argue that the Gospels tell us nothing of Jesus' tone of voice or the look in his eyes or his body language. Too often, in mistaken piety, we ignore his manifest sense of humour. Equally, he may have felt constrained to warn about the possibility of eternal separation from God, but the thought of it may have caused him heartbreaking anguish, as did his vision of the fate awaiting Jerusalem. For the most part the Gospel writers were not interested in supplying the sort of psychological clues we demand.

Nor can we take for granted that every detail of their presentations of Jesus is reliable as pure record. They differ too much. Matthew, for instance, gives far more prominence to teaching on hell than do any of the others. All four paint Jesus with the eye of faith. We rightly insist that faith is rooted in fact, but we have to accept that Jesus exactly as he was will always elude us.

Yet though these qualifications may be justified, to be always on the defensive, permanently apologising, is no way either to preach the Good News or to build up in ourselves a lively faith. Such caveats are but footnotes, and must never be promoted to being the main text of our story of Jesus. One thing that will help us avoid that mistake is to take seriously God's vindication of Jesus in the resurrection, and to rethink our idea of sinlessness.

Sin, we are told by theologians, is 'deliberate disobedience to the known will of God'. But that can make the quest for sinlessness a rather negative thing – playing safe by trying to avoid any breach of God's rules. That was how the Scribes understood it when, for example, they called Jesus a sinner for breaking the regulations governing the Sabbath. But Jesus appealed beyond the rules to a deeper understanding of the will of God. When God freed us from routine work on the Sabbath, that was freedom to restore and enrich life, to give love full rein, not to do nothing.

For Jesus, 'doing the will of God' could never be adequately compassed by avoiding what God forbade. It was a positive concept: doing to the maximum what God wanted in every situation. 'My food,' he says, 'is to do the will of him who sent me, and to finish his work.'

Jesus bursts on the scene in Palestine with clamorous urgency. 'Repent, the kingdom of God is upon you!' It is as if he has been pent up for thirty years, but has at last seen clearly what his life is for, and that it may be even now too late to do all he has to do. He moves at top speed from town to town. He prays during the night on the mountains, because the days are precious time when the people can be reached and healed. So he keeps the crowds out all day, teaching as if he would never have another chance. The pressure is so great that at times he and his disciples cannot even snatch a bite to eat.

What Jesus saw as at stake in this mission was nothing less than the fate of Israel and the fulfilment of her God-given destiny to be the light of the world. The two major forces in society – the religious establishment and the revolutionary men of violence – were equally, if in different ways, blocking her from carrying out God's will.

Crisis point could come at any time. It was too late for polite diplomacy or leisured education. The only way was the way of the prophet, whose voice always angers but can never be ignored.

Dedication to God's overriding command leaves little room for the niceties of conventional behaviour – how often do the lives of the saints warn us of that! That is what the story of the young Jesus in the Temple foreshadows. When discovered, he does not apologise, quite the opposite: 'Why did you have to search for me? Didn't you realise I was bound to be in my Father's house?' The needful ruthlessness is already showing. Perhaps the most remarkable thing about Mary, his mother, is that she seems to have known intuitively that things had to be this way. 'Whatever he tells you, do it,' she says to the servants at Cana. With other women, friends and relatives, she goes along throughout his mission, keeping the show on the road, the winding road to Calvary.

In this she offers us a crucial lesson. Many things we are quick to call signs of sinfulness are nothing of the kind. They are signs of the rickety machinery of our species, which does not always operate as others would prefer. But part of the service love is called to give is to nullify the potential evil in our conduct to one another by not making a court case of such things, but letting the exasperation slide away. True, we all have a general duty to act sensitively toward the needs and vulnerabilities of others – that is part of the Golden Rule and of loving our neighbour as ourself. To reject that duty would indeed be sinful, but no one can fairly accuse Jesus of that.

We should keep the word 'sin' for the big things – the hatred, envy, greed, injustice, malice, hedonism, egocentricity, contempt for other people and other creatures, and most of all the cruelty – which allow evil to extend its empire at the expense of the kingdom of heaven. But who can convict Jesus of these things?

No one, and why not? Because his mind and heart were preoccupied not with his own goodness (remember what he said to the rich young ruler, 'Why do you call me good? No one is good but God') but with the urgent promotion of God's priorities: care for the sick and outcast, the rejection of violence and the reign of forgiveness, awakening people to their own cant and self-righteousness, and staying with these things even to the point of a horrible and seemingly futile death.

This was the sinlessness which Easter vindicated. The only way to empty our own lives of evil is, like Jesus, to fill them with positive good, the particular vision and action, suffering and love which the Spirit reveals through prayer as God's priorities today.

It was first of all in the contacts Jesus made with men and women; Peter hauling in his net after a night's fishing; Martha bustling in and out of her kitchen; the centurion puzzled and sad about his servant, that he showed them the application of his teaching. Because of what he was to them, 'that which we have heard, that which we have seen with our eyes, that which we beheld, and our hands have handled, concerning the Word of life', they knew God was love.

Harold S. Darby

It is only when we are prepared to let Jesus take his rightful place as Master and Lord of our whole life, that we can realise the fulfilment of the prayer, 'Now the God of peace himself give you peace always by all means.' We shall know them, by a blessed and abiding experience, what the peace of Jesus really is, and share with him the peace which he shared with the Father from before the foundation of the world.

Thomas Cook

Travelling on with Jesus

Wendy Craig

What a strange, topsy-turvy profession show business is! As an actress I often go to work when everybody else seems to be coming home, I eat at the most extraordinary times, and I finally slump into bed well after the rest of the country has put its lights out. As I go from working in a London television studio, to twelve shows a week in pantomime in Wales, and then on a theatre tour across country, I am reminded that every day in my life is different; nothing is constant.

How much more important, then, that my Christian faith provides the stability I need to exist and function as a human being. The God I discovered as a child all those years ago loved me enough to walk with me hand in hand, day by day, moment by moment. It's extraordinary to think that, even though I let go of his hand for many years, he never left my side, but waited patiently for me to turn and acknowledge him as central to my life once more.

Jesus was constant in his care of others. He was always ready to listen: to a small boy offering his packed lunch, or to a Jewish leader visiting him in secret. Not that he didn't have a few surprises for those around him – Jesus was never predictable. When one disciple urged him to come and heal those in need Jesus went in the opposite direction, and when everybody thought he was dead and finished, he sprang back to life!

When I look at the Gospels, the life of Jesus provides a wonderful example for me. As a creative person, I would probably be hopeless in any other career than that which stretches my ability as a performer. This involves different jobs, various venues and diverse roles. When I am at home I love to fall into an everyday routine of eating at normal times, inviting friends to dinner and walking in the countryside. What gives me the greatest security is that whether I am on the move or whether I am at home, God is with me.

Jesus was constantly 'on the move', yet always available. He travelled far and wide, and handled the demands that his fame brought upon him, yet he was always prepared to stop and enjoy hospitality along the way. So it is with God. He didn't just create the world and then sit down to let humanity get on with it alone. He is continually involved, his work both seen and unseen.

In my stop-and-start world, I hold on to the promise that God is constant. He is never too busy to hear my plea for help; he is never away on holiday and unable to guide me; he is never asleep and too tired to wrap his arms around me. It doesn't matter where I am either; God is not like a mobile telephone that is out of range in certain places. He is there by my side, on-stage and off, every moment of the day, never intrusive but always there.

'Like father, like son,' we often say. So it was with Jesus. He showed what God the Father is like. When Hebrews announces that he is 'the same yesterday, today and forever', it doesn't mean that Jesus is boring and uncreative. On the contrary this verse illustrates that despite the fact that he walks with us in the ups and downs of our lives, his character is forever and totally dependable. In a changing world, and a changing profession, I can trust the character of an unchanging God. What a relief!

Jesus spent a lot of time walking with others during his short time on earth. When he encountered the Pharisees and others who sought to trick him, he could be relied upon for a sharp reply. When he met those in genuine need, whose hearts and lives were open, he never failed to meet their expectations of him through healing and wisdom. Jesus was concerned more with relationships than with dogma, regulations or politics.

Beside the disciples who benefited greatly from Jesus' involvement in their interminable discussions, there were people like the woman at the well. As a woman I just love to see the way in which Jesus treated the opposite sex. Their society put them down, and robbed them of so much dignity, yet Jesus was in the business of replacing this with respect and value. In the Gospels every person who met him went away with a story to tell, but few more so than this Samaritan woman.

When she admitted that she was not living her life as she knew she should, Jesus did not rant and rave at her, nor use a fine preaching opportunity to underline where she had got it wrong. Instead, he offered her a drink of his living water, which he promised would satisfy her inner thirst for the rest of her life. The transformation he recommended came from the inside out, and astounded her so much that she ran to tell all her neighbours.

I often get it wrong, but when I do, I need never be afraid that as I approach God looking for forgiveness that he will get out his big stick and hit me. Like the father in Jesus' story of the prodigal son he runs towards me with open arms. God's care for me is predictable and the demands that he places on my life are reachable; he never insists on more than I am able to give.

Someone once said that God is never disillusioned with us, as he never has illusions about us in the first place! He knows exactly what we are made of, what we are capable of and how best to lead us forward.

God does not restrict himself to being with me only on my good days, or when I am at my happiest. Nor does he avoid me when I'm grumpy, or stressed. No matter where I am, or how I am feeling, God wants to build a relationship with me that is not dependent on how good I am, but relies on his grace alone.

It's also fantastic that God doesn't get 'off days' when he just can't be bothered to listen to my problems. He doesn't get a headache or retire early to bed, or get so temperamental with me that he decides not to love me any more. Not only is God constant in his availability, he is constant in his character too.

What can I rely on these days? Change happens so quickly, I don't even notice it sometimes. What I can be certain of is God's love for me. His availability and patience assure me that one day I shall live with him in eternity. His promises, just like God himself, are reliable, and in a world that is constantly changing, it's all I need.

*Christians have claimed down the centuries that
Jesus shows the real God to us as fully as it is
possible for us to understand. The Christian
Scriptures are the record of those who believed this
to be so and wanted to tell other people about their
discovery. They tell of people who found their
answer to the question, 'How can I know God?'
when they met Jesus. They had a glimpse of God in
the flesh in another person, and they fell down and
worshipped him. They also tell of people who passed
this experience on to others who were not personally
present, and who found they could understand and
believe.*

Maurice Friggens

Jesus is to us a true index of what God is, and of what we
may be, and (in God's thought of us) are meant to be. It is
not only in things Jesus said and did that this revelation of
God and of ourselves is given, but even more in all that he
himself was in his entire relationship and dealing with
God, in the nature of his response to God, and in the whole
quality of his spirit and service.

John T. Brewis

Now with the special gift of imagination, picture yourself approaching the crowd around Jesus. You long to get through to him about someone you love. Now see the crowd and the open corridor directly to the Lord made for you. He is there for you. Now stand before him, face to face, heart to heart. He is waiting for you to ask for what he is ready to give. Tell him about a person or persons on your heart. Then wait for his answer. At this very moment you prayed, says Jesus, my power has been released in the person for whom you interceded. My will shall be done, in my timing, according to my plan, and for the now and forever blessing of your loved one. You and I are of one heart now. We both love and care. Now go your way in faithfulness.

Lloyd John Ogilvie

O Christ, our only Saviour,
So dwell within us
That we may go forth
With the light of hope in our eyes,
And the fire of inspiration on our lips,
Thy word on our tongues,
And thy love in our hearts.

Selina F. Fox

Let us quietly recall the grace of our Lord Jesus,
who lived royally in a humble cottage,
who knew how to find God's power in the silence of prayer,
who saw the wonder of God in the wayside lilies;
whose love made simple disciples into loyal apostles,
who rebuked all shams and hypocrisies,
who endured shame and misunderstanding and loneliness,
who suffered and died to free us from the fetter of sin.

O come to our hearts, Lord Jesus;
There is room in our hearts for thee.

Anonymous

Christ turned the world's accepted standards upside down. It was the poor, not the rich, who were to be blessed; the weak, not the strong, who were to be esteemed; the pure in heart, not the sophisticated and the worldly, who understood what life was about. We should love our enemies, bless them that curse us, do good to them that hate us, and pray for them that despitefully use us, in order that we may be worthy members of a human family whose Father is in heaven.

So Christ spoke. No one has fully carried out his sublime behests, but it is due to his words . . . that some, at least, have tried.

Malcolm Muggeridge

[Jesus] seems really to have liked his disreputable friends and to have found among them a sincerity and openness to the realities of life that are often lacking among those whose existence has been cushioned against those harsh realities. He was prepared to accept them in their pathetic absurdity, their alienation from society, and the darkening of their minds and spirits. They could not wear out his patience; stupid, inconstant and faithless, they found him changeless and always the same. He was prepared to trust them even when they were not worthy of any trust.

Stephen Neill

Jesus meant no encouragement to idleness when he said that God who fed the sparrows and clothed the lilies would feed and clothe us. Sparrows in fact work hard for their food. Yet it is God who feeds them, and when they die it is not without the Father, as Jesus said. Nor was Jesus discouraging reasonable forethought and planning when he told us not to worry about tomorrow. Anxious fears about what we cannot control are not the same as thought and planning for the common good.

Hugh Martin

Make us wise, O Lord, to reverence that which is worthy;
and having seen the pearl of great price,
to desire it above all things,
and with glad heart to surrender all else,
if only we may thereby obtain it.
For thy name's sake. Amen.

Anonymous, 17th century

The Present Christ

David Adam

I often begin a church service with the words 'The Lord is here' and the congregation responds, 'His Spirit is with us.' I wonder how many people really mean what they are saying, that our God is present and with us? Do we take to heart the last words of Jesus in Matthew's Gospel, 'I am with you always'? It is of the utmost importance to our faith that we learn to relax in the presence and enjoy the company of our Lord. Our Lord is alive and gives us an opportunity of having a relationship with him.

As a young choirboy I learnt texts of the Scriptures by singing anthems. Our choirmaster was a perfectionist; we had to sing the same words over and over again until he felt they were absolutely right. The words that were for ever to stick in my mind and heart were 'Rejoice in the Lord always, and again, I say, rejoice.' It would be years before I knew that those words came from Philippians 4, but I took them to heart: I learnt to rejoice in the Lord, in his love, in his presence.

In Advent and leading up to Christmas, I like to pray, 'Lord come down, come in, come among us.' I do not think the words make God come, for that would be magic. God is always with us; if he were not with us we would not exist. In such prayers I am opening myself up to the God who comes, who is ever present among us. The Christ I worship and love is not a figure of history; though he was that, he is the living Lord and present with me at each moment. Christ is not a person from the past, he is here now and he eternally gives himself for us and to us. The Christ who is, is to be met and conversed with. He is

not a theory about life or about God; he is not even
to be studied as much as to be encountered. The C
the one we should talk to rather than talk about. Th
too many groups who are willing to theorise an
about the Christ but rarely spend much time talki ᵕ ᴥ
him. Such groups often confuse faith with credal
statements and their own reasoning. Faith is more than
belief, it is to have a living personal relationship with God.
Faith is not so much believing as knowing in the sense of
being personally involved with God. Devils can believe in
God, but they do not have faith.

When I was a child I loved the picture puzzles that had
hidden faces in the trees, in the bushes and in the
landscape, faces that you would see only if you took your
time and looked carefully. In much the same way the
hidden presence of Christ is there to be found in his world.
We cannot imagine this presence, for he is there, but we
can attune ourselves to be more aware. This is not about
feelings, for feelings can be liars, nor is it positive thinking
for some of that can be positively stupid. It is about
reality. The Lord is here, and it is how we react to this fact
that shows our faith. It is no use saying we believe if we
ignore our God.

I believe it is good to affirm the fact of the presence, to
remind ourselves and attune ourselves. Among my daily
prayers, I always have prayers of affirmation, for such
prayer helps to awaken my dull senses. I say such prayers
as the prayer attributed to St Patrick:

> Christ as a light,
> Illumine and guide me!
> Christ as a shield overshadow me and cover me!
> Christ be under me! Christ be over me!
> Christ beside me, on left hand and right!
> Christ be before me, behind me, about me!
> Christ this day be within and without me!
> Christ the lowly and meek,
> Christ the all-powerful be

> In the heart of each to whom I speak,
> In the mouth of each who speaks to me,
> In all who draw near me,
> Or see me, or hear me!

This is not to make the Christ do any of this, but to make me aware that he is already doing all of this. It is to open my eyes to the Christ who is, who is here, who is with us now. If we do not spend time enjoying his presence, abiding in his company, we may believe but we are lacking in faith, for faith is the vital, living relationship. Stop talking about him and get to know him. Check your own attitude to Christ – do you talk more of what he has done, or what he is doing? Is your Christ a present Christ with whom you have to do? Learn to speak directly to him. Say such words as:

> You, Lord, are in this place
> Your presence fills it
> Your presence is joy . . .

Repeat this prayer, changing the end word to 'love', 'light', 'peace', or changing the ending of the first line to 'in this church', 'in this wood', 'in my heart'. I like to end this affirmation by slowly getting rid of too many words, and enjoy the presence:

> You, Lord, are in this place
> You, Lord, are
> You, Lord
> You

I have discovered that the Christ often reveals himself to us in the other person; he is to be found in the friend and stranger. If we are unwilling to accept the otherness of another person, how shall we begin to learn of the Great Other who is God? If we do not allow otherness to break into our lives and rules, we are in danger of fencing God out. God comes to us in the other. Christ is to be met in each and every one with whom we meet.

When I was doing theology at College, I had a crisis of faith – perhaps that is what theology is meant to bring about! Whilst I was struggling with the complexities of dogma and the 'problems' of the 'Word made flesh', I felt I was missing out on the reality of it all. Fortunately we were asked to go to worship seven times a day and the secret lay there. What the mind could not grasp, the heart could hold. God was not a problem to be solved but a mystery to be enjoyed. In this struggle I came across these words and found them to express a deep reality:

> I sought my God, my God I could not see;
> I sought my soul, my soul eluded me;
> I sought my brother – I found all three.

In being open and attentive to others, I was able to become more open and attentive to God. I have learnt that God speaks often through the other who comes to me. I must respect every person, for in them I encounter the Christ. Wherever there is any sense of meeting, he is there. There is no doubt that Christ comes to each of us. Let us make room for him.

Too often we seek his gifts when we should be seeking to know his presence. The grace of our Lord Jesus Christ is all that he gives to us. His greatest gift of all is that he gives himself to us.

The Lord is with you.

Through Jesus people heard God speak, and in him they saw God at work, revealing himself. Jesus had the value of God for those nearest to him; and this, despite his protests. In him they saw the Father, because God was so manifestly *there*. In Jesus, they later claimed, they began to see and touch, to understand and trust, that 'Word', or 'Wisdom' – God's perfect plan for us – that had been always in the heart of the Father. The secret was now out; gloriously revealed, in this most human of men, Jesus.

David Francis

It was the New Testament which really awakened me to the rightness and value of passive resistance, and love towards one's enemies. When I read in the Sermon on the Mount such passages: 'Resist not him that is evil, but whosoever smiteth thee in thy right cheek, turn to him the other also'; or 'love your enemies, bless them that persecute you, that you may be the sons of your Father which is in heaven', I was simply overjoyed.

Mahatma Gandhi

I am led to repose in places of quiet, before being guided to strenuous action. In any service done by faith in his name Christ lovingly lights the path. Whenever through wilfulness I turn prodigal he is always awaiting my return. When I cannot see his face because of sudden darkness of sorrow, lack of understanding or sin, if I hold fast to my faith, in time I see more clearly and trustingly than before.

Marjorie Wilkinson

He did not overthrow the oppressive government of Rome. He did not lower the tax rate. He did not improve sanitary conditions in Jerusalem, nor erect a public library at Nazareth . . . He taught no sure cure for disease. The economic status of his followers was exactly as it had been; he found them fishermen, he left them fishermen . . . But his fishermen were different – endowed with power, capable of great faith and magnificent achievement.

Bruce Barton

Christ, you are calling.
In the hated,
in the hopeless,
in the helpless,
in the haunted,
you are waiting for me.

Christ, you are calling.
In the homeless,
in the stranger,
in the children,
in me,
you are waiting for me.

I want to follow you, Christ Jesus,
so when you call,
help me to hear your voice,
when you beckon,
help me not to look back.
In the face of the familiar
strengthen my commitment
and make me fit for your kingdom.

Francis Brienen

Lord, whose love through humble service
Bore the weight of human need,
Who upon the cross, forsaken,
Offered mercy's perfect deed:
We, your servants, bring the worship
Not of voice alone, but heart,
Consecrating to your purpose
Every gift that you impart.

Still your children wander homeless;
Still the hungry cry for bread;
Still the captives long for freedom;
Still in grief we mourn our dead.
As, O Lord, your deep compassion
Healed the sick and freed the soul,
Use the love your spirit kindles
Still to save and make us whole.

As we worship, grant us vision,
Till your love's revealing light
In its height and depth and greatness
Dawns upon our quickened sight,
Making known the needs and burdens
Your compassion bids us bear,
Stirring us to tireless striving
Your abundant life to share.

Called by worship to your service,
Forth in your dear name we go
To the child, the youth, the aged,
Love in living deeds to show;
Hope and health, goodwill and comfort,
Counsel, aid and peace we give,
That your servants, Lord, in freedom
May your mercy know, and live.

Albert Frederick Bayly

What makes an experience religious is the way in which it is taken by the subject. Thus, to St Paul stripes, stones, shipwrecks, and thorns in the flesh were religious experiences, while to Judas Iscariot the daily companionship of Jesus of Nazareth was not. The non-Christian will find Christ never and nowhere; the saints will find him at all times and in all things.

Leonard Hodgson

I owned a little boat a while ago,
And sailed the morning sea without a fear,
And whither any breeze might fairly blow,
I sailed my little craft afar or near.
Mine was the boat,
And mine the air,
And mine the sea,
Not mine a care.

My boat became my place of mighty toil,
I sailed at evening to the fishing ground.
At morn my boat was freighted with the spoil
Which my all-conquering work had found.
Mine was the boat
And mine the net,
And mine the skill
And power to get.

Once from the boat he taught the curious throng,
Then bade me cast my net into the sea;
I murmured, but obeyed, nor was it long
Before the catch amazed and humbled me.
His was the boat,
And his the skill,
And his the catch,
And his my will.

George Macdonald

Son of God, Son of Man

James Thompson

When I was asked to write on this awesome title, I was in a state of physical collapse with a back problem. Ironically this gave me a deeper opportunity to explore the subject in a personal way. To experience something of the wilderness and isolation of being in continuous pain and bedridden gave me, in a small way, an idea of what many people have to live with for years, a taste of 'the dark night of the soul'. Though this was relatively minor suffering, it seemed a lot to me! I realised how precious it was to see in Jesus a human person, who, like us, faced life's changes and chances.

Jesus was born in the human stream of oppressed people, he experienced temptation as we do, was isolated and ridiculed and, on the night of his arrest, threw himself headlong on the ground and was deeply distressed and troubled: 'My soul is overwhelmed with sorrow to the point of death.' Then, in a moment of raw humanity: 'My God, my God, why have you forsaken me?' – not only passages from Jewish prayers, but also a universal cry of the human race. Then, like us all, he experienced dying and death. But his humanness was not only in his suffering, it was in the laughter, the love, the enjoyment of nature, the love of children, his compassion and his love for God whom he called 'Abba', that so human expression of a child's love for his father. All these profound signs of his humanity are sources of hope and comfort, and were to me at my lowest moments.

Alongside this shared humanity, I also felt a deep need for something beyond the human. It's a very basic yearning for the strength of God to restore or prevent the loss of a quality of life through some transcendent power. Just as Jesus, in his own life, turned aside to pray to God and recognised the healing power of God, so too I found the necessity to be open to the 'Godness' of God, and began to see that, though the Gospels constantly show us the humanness of Jesus Christ, the light of the heavenly dimension also repeatedly shines through. We glimpse there the supernatural setting of Jesus' human story and are encouraged to believe in the heavenly environment of our own journey.

Heaven breaks through in the angels' music at Jesus' birth, in the voice of God at his baptism, the power over the demons, in the witness of the apostles –'You are the Christ, the Son of the living God' – and, most movingly in Thomas, seeing the risen Christ, finally able to say, 'My Lord and my God'. From beginning to end the Gospel stories are about the Son of Man and the Son of God, and the ascension to heaven was the way the disciples described Christ's returning to share the glory of God, the creator of the universe, the great Spirit of all life. When we look at Jesus' life, death, resurrection and ascension we see the human and the divine integrated by the Gospel writers into an amazing unity which cannot be divided up into human bits and divine bits. In the weakness of illness I needed to see through Jesus, our Brother and Companion, to Jesus, God from God, light from light.

This indivisible unity led to the church finally defining Jesus as truly human and truly divine. This issue was the cause of the greatest divisions in the early church. There were those who denied the divinity of Jesus, who claimed like Islam that he was a great prophet but not Son of God and certainly not 'God from God'. There were others who wanted so much to preserve his divinity that they claimed he didn't really suffer in the Garden, that there were no limitations on his human knowledge, and that on the cross his divinity escaped and mocked those who crucified him.

But why, we might ask, was it such a problem to the church?

It's important for us to see it is a real question. It's partly a matter of our imagination, and partly the insistent demand of religious need. Can we imagine how the majestic creator, the author of the Big Bang, the almighty, unchanging, eternal, 'immortal, invisible, in light inaccessible' can also become a human being? How can this God, in whose mind all creation evolved, become a man however good, however just, however loving? Can we imagine this God like us, changing his mind, experiencing pain, crying because of the tears of things? It's not only difficult to imagine, it also seems to undermine the power so needed to be found in God.

If God is changeable, suffering, susceptible to weakness, then how can we rely on him? Such people said, 'Son of Man' – yes, like other prophets, maybe even unique in virtue and vision, but 'Son of God' was a big step too far. They could not accept St Paul's teaching in Colossians: 'He is the image of the invisible God . . . In him all the fullness of God was pleased to dwell.' The gap for many people between the human and divine could not be bridged. This division within the church kept on recurring, but its eventual affirmation of the integrated divinity and humanity of Christ is to be seen in the creeds finalised at Nicaea and Chalcedon.

In my illness I began to understand a little better how it is possible to see the relationship between the humanity and divinity of Jesus. It evolves from the definition St John gives us of God, that God is love. At the heart of our Christian faith is the prayer which begins 'Our Father . . . ' Loving parents have an enormous amount of feeling for their children in their minds and hearts, which might issue in a stern yet forgiving word. They might experience fear for their children, cry for their children, hug their children – none of which diminishes but rather expresses the love they feel. Love does not have to be almighty to be worthwhile; in fact, in some ways 'almightyness' can be a contradiction of love, because God longs for the free response of his children.

It is the love in God which can absorb the pain, the change, the grief, and even, we are taught by Jesus Christ, the sin of humanity. If the category of love is applied to the humanity and the divinity it no longer seems to me like an impossible step to travel from that Man to that God. The kingdom of love is distinct from the kingdom of earthly power, and it is the kingdom of love we are called to seek. The more we see that love is the defining characteristic of God and his Son, Jesus Christ, the less we shall be bogged down in arguments about trying to separate the humanity and the divinity.

Because of our very rational, scientific modes of thought we have found it increasingly difficult to use the wonderful pictures of the heavenly dimension to be found in the Bible, and many people find the supernatural elements of the life of Jesus Christ to be embarrassing. But in our generation we need to hold very firmly on to the Son of God as well as the Son of Man. To do otherwise would dilute the Gospel itself.

The deeper we go into God, the more we shall have to draw on pictures and myths to help us to touch the hem of God's being; to look deeper into the divinity as well as the humanity of Christ is to study the God-given image of God himself. This has big implications for our prayers. The love of Jesus, which is the focus of so much of our prayers, is a gate of heaven, a way for our consciousness to become open to the truth, beauty and unspeakable wonder of the love of God himself. We travel with our brother, our hearts burning within us, to the mystery of heaven, where Jesus Christ, Son of Man, Son of God, sits on the throne at the right hand of the Father in glory.

Hope of the world, thou Christ of great compassion,
Speak to our fearful hearts by conflict rent.
Save us, thy people, from consuming passion,
Who by our own false hopes and aims are spent.

Hope of the world, God's gift from highest heaven,
Bringing to hungry souls the bread of life,
Still let thy spirit unto us be given,
To heal earth's wounds and end all bitter strife.

Hope of the world, afoot on dusty highways,
Showing to wandering souls the path of light,
Walk thou beside us lest the tempting byways
Lure us away from thee to endless night.

Hope of the world, who by the cross didst save us
From death and dark despair, from sin and guilt,
We render back the love thy mercy gave us;
Take thou our lives, and use them as thou wilt.

Hope of the world, O Christ o'er death victorious,
Who by this sign didst conquer grief and pain,
We would be faithful to thy Gospel glorious;
Thou art our Lord! Thou dost forever reign.

Georgia Harkness

Luke set it down in simple words: 'He went about doing good.' His feet, sandal-shod, often dusty and weary, took him amongst men and women with common needs. This enabled him to pause a moment beside a well, as he journeyed, to talk with a woman of Samaria; they took him with all haste to the side of Mary and Martha in their grief; they led him at last steadfastly toward Jerusalem and to the crowning task of his life.

Rita Snowden

There is no one else who is seriously bidding for the heart of the world except Jesus Christ. There is no one else on the field.

Anonymous

We praise you, O God, for the courage, the gentleness, and the unselfishness of Christ. We remember with gratitude that in the face of danger he continued his work without flinching, that he used his great powers of mind and body never arrogantly, but always with gentleness and consideration, that he never sought his own gain or advancement, but always worked for the strengthening and encouragement of others. Grant us so to live, by your Spirit of power enabling us, that we may follow Christ loyally and so become daily more like him. Amen.

Rupert Davies

Prayer is something more than that which we do with our minds. It also involves our hearts and spirits – that deeper part of our personalities to which only the Spirit of Jesus has access. Prayer in its highest form requires more than conscious effort. It also requires the surrender of our innermost selves to Jesus, giving him permission to make our lives a continually flowing fountain of unceasing prayer. When we have learned how to do that, we will have discovered the secret of the prayer of the heart.

Robert V. Dodd

Even for Jesus himself, whose fellowship with his Father was so constant, there had to be nights of prayer and the times apart. His disciples felt the contrast between being with him and facing the world, not only on the classic occasion of his Transfiguration and its sequel, but on many other occasions. One thinks of Peter's radiant confession of faith and declaration of loyalty in the presence of Christ, and his sad denial of him before others.

Clive Thexton

The God of constant, everlasting love, the God of abiding covenant and of truth appears in Jesus Christ. He stands out in striking contrast to an uncertain world. The devil cannot move him. The entrenched opinions of Pharisees and Sadducees cannot unsettle him. In spite of the certain prospect of death he sets his face steadfastly to go to Jerusalem.

Wilfred Easton

God in Jesus, who created the universe with its incomprehensible vastness and its millions of years of teeming life – wept (John 11:35) . . . What was the meaning of those tears? Tears are shocking, unanswerable, compelling; they are inadequate. As I try to visualise those two scenes of weeping I see Jesus' divinity and his humanity in sharp tension. He loved his friend Lazarus and those two so disparate sisters. His friend was dead, the sisters inconsolable in their grief . . . They were tears of human love, compassion and empathy, but surely they were also divine tears, tears of frustration flowing from the eternal God who is concerned for the death of a sparrow, and at the limited understanding of his friends, locked in their little time-warp.

John Williams

'Let not your hearts be troubled.' Comfort is not in silence or in words; it is in Jesus – in a vastly heightened sense of his nearness and his truth. This is the open secret of the untroubled heart. There are those who have shrunk from the very contemplation of living on in a world bereft of some dearly loved one, or have tried in vain to shut their minds to the realisation of some awful possibility. But if at last they have cried out in pain and utter despair, 'Master, master', they have learned something of the deep mystery of how the heavenly comfort is administered, for it is no less than the gifts of himself.

Frank C. Eden

Jesus, Giver of Release

Flora Slosson Wuellner

I woke, the dungeon flamed with light;
My chains fell off, my heart was free,
I rose, went forth, and followed thee.

Charles Wesley

When I was twelve years old my grandmother died in our home of a sudden, massive heart attack. She had lived with us since I was a baby, and we were close, loving friends. She had taught me so many beautiful things about nature, art, poetry, and as a child I assumed she would always be there.

We were all shocked awake by her sudden illness and in the confusion of the running footsteps, telephones ringing, doctors arriving, I crept into my bedroom closet, shut the door firmly behind me, and sat in the dark on top of my shoes. I was not really conscious of shock and grief, but only numbness. All I wanted to do was to sit there alone in the safe dark and never come out.

Suddenly I felt someone there with me in the closet. Though I neither saw nor heard anything, and the door remained shut, there was definitely a Presence, close, silent, loving. Then I felt as if strong, tender hands enfolded mine and I was gently pulled to my feet. Powerful warmth flooded my body, and I opened the door and stepped out.

That was the first time the living Christ released me from enclosing doors, but it has happened many times since.

Repeatedly I have been brought out of the enclosed defences of shyness, timidity, withdrawal, avoidance of others and the adventures of life. Most of the time these inner releases have not come with the sense of a supernatural Presence, but looking back I realise it has always been the liberating hand of the risen Christ, who could never endure leaving 'the spirits in prison' (1 Peter 3:19).

I can think of no spiritual leader in history who so deeply, radically, passionately sought to release the human spirit from its bondage and prisons both individual and communal. He boldly proclaimed his mission when he came forth from the desert of temptation and in the Nazareth synagogue read from the prophet Isaiah:

> He has sent me to proclaim release to the captives,
> and recovery of sight to the blind,
> to let the oppressed go free,
> to proclaim the year of the Lord's favour.

Luke 4:18, 19

Jesus refers pointedly to the 'year of the Lord's favour', which was the 'Year of Jubilee'. Every fifty years in Israel (at least theoretically) the curved ram's horn, the Shofar, was to be blown throughout the land to proclaim a year of release and rest. All slaves were to be set free, all debtors forgiven their debts, all captives released from prison. Even the land was to be released to a year of rest, fallowness.

When Jesus concluded his reading by saying: 'Today this scripture has been fulfilled in your hearing' (Luke 4:21) he meant that God at that very moment blew the Shofar of release through Jesus, opening the prison doors, sounding through our bodies, minds, spirits.

How often his miracles were acts not only of healing but also release. We can understand his miracles on three levels: first, to heal the person in front of him from illness, pain, death; second, to show by such healing that this was the nature of God's kingdom; third, to release the whole community present from its spiritual prisons.

For example, when he healed the bent woman (Luke 13:10-17) certainly her release from years of impediment was vital to him, but equally important was the release of the people of her town from their burden of rigid rules that were put ahead of mercy.

It is fascinating to read the Gospels observing how Jesus sought in every way to release others from their bondages, addictions, spiritual constrictions. It was, of course, these acts and words of release that aroused such hostility and suspicion against him that he was considered too dangerous to be allowed to live.

During the Last Supper, Jesus looked around at his disciples and said, with astounding implication: 'I do not call you servants any longer . . . I have called you friends' (John 15:15). With these words he takes us all, his disciples then and now, forever out of the master-servant, dominance-submission, conquest-surrender relationship with God, which has been the source of so much spiritual abuse through the centuries. Jesus brings us into a way of relating to God and one another in which mutual serving is not that of servants, but of the beloved.

But Jesus also said earlier in that passage: 'This is my commandment, that you love one another as I have loved you' (v12). Does this word return us back again into the realm of submission and disempowerment? How can one command a beloved friend?

The root meaning of the word 'command' comes from the Latin word 'mandus' meaning 'the hand', from which we also get our word 'mandate'. In ancient times a rod of authority was put into the hand of a general or delegate which empowered him to act in the name of the delegator and backed up by the full powers of the delegator. When Jesus gave his command, his mandate to live the life of love, he was saying: 'I empower you to live the life of love in my name, and I promise to sustain you in this life with my abiding presence, even as the vine empowers and sustains the branch.' For in Christ, we are released from a hierarchical spiritual life of greater down to lesser, into a holographic spiritual life in which the whole abides in each of the parts.

Have we heard and understood these words of Jesus? Why do so many of our theologies, our forms of spirituality, our methodologies, our liturgies, our hymns still reflect the bondage relationship with God rather than the bonding – its exact opposite?

It is a major tragedy of religious history that most spiritual movements and reforms which began by releasing the spirit become themselves new prisons of the spirit with rigid, divisive rules and walls. In our personal spiritual lives, so often a method or discipline that originally released us to new freedom within God has become an imprisoning idolatry of that system itself. We begin to worship the rule rather than the living God.

Often, when caught up in an enthusiasm for some new spiritual teaching, method, leader or community, I need to remind myself of those profoundly releasing words of King Solomon as he dedicated his magnificent, painstakingly-built temple to God: 'Even heaven and the highest heaven cannot contain you, much less this house that I have built!' (1 Kings 8:27). God is free, and we are made in God's image.

From what inner prisons does God long to release each of us? It takes much honesty to discern what it is in our lives that makes us unfree, holds us down, bends us over, boxes us in. Is our inner prison an addiction? A destructive habit? Submission to an abuse relationship? Idolatry of some system or community? A life dominated by fear and guilt? An inherited generational wound and burden? An unhealed grief or trauma? A smouldering resentment? A fear of closeness and commitment? A need to dominate and control? Learning to listen to our bodies (our deepest truth-tellers and spiritual directors) tells us much about our inner 'unfreedoms', both spiritual and emotional. Sharing these questions with trusted friends and counsellors may deepen our healing and give the reassurance, encouragement and guidance that all prisoners need when set free.

How essential it is to know that God was with us all along in our inner prisons! The powerful scripture in which Jesus encounters his disciples for the first time after his resurrection (John 20:19-22) has been a revelation to me for many years. In fear and guilt his disciples sat behind locked doors on the night of the resurrection. Jesus did not break down the door, for the God we see through Jesus is not an assaulter. Our fears and defences that rise from our wounds are understood by God, who heals our doors and masks rather than tearing them down. (In the same way we should never invade or assault the defences of others in the name of liberation!) Nevertheless, the risen Jesus came through the shut door (even as he came to me), stood among them without condemnation, gave them the word of Shalom, which means wholeness, shared his wounds with them, breathed on them the empowering breath of his Holy Spirit, all before that door was unlocked!

As they felt released in their deepest selves, they opened the door and went forth to lives of empowered love, releasing and healing others in the sustaining Presence.

Yes, that is the next question, of course. God not only releases us from something but also to something. As the healing deepens, the gifts and powers unfold. What lies ahead? John tells us: 'Beloved, we are God's children now;

what we will be has not yet been revealed' (1 John 3:2). That is merciful. Could the acorn endure seeing the magnitude of the full oak tree that lies within it? Again, God is not an assaulter. Each step we take towards the heights will be as a homecoming, for the heights dwell within us already.

On that morning long ago as I looked at my grandmother's still face, it was enough at that moment to know that I had not been alone in that dark closet, that God's love empowered me to turn the handle and open the door, that my beloved grandmother and I were both released into a wider life of love, and that 'what will be' was in God's hands.

Jesus gave this law of love . . . when he enjoined his disciples at the Last Supper to 'love one another as I have loved you'. This is not a simple thing to do for Jesus' love was radically self-giving. To be a Christian then means not only that you are a recipient of this awesome gift but that you must incarnate this radical love yourself. You must become transformed by and into the love manifested by Jesus Christ.

Wendy M. Wright

The world's destiny is concentrated on a towel, while a baleful world outside is preparing a trial and a cross. Point and counterpoint, dark and light, matched together reveal the truth. God's purpose lies over the whole; the tug of evil is at the very heart of the embryo church; Caiaphas is sleepless through hate; ignorant soldiers are being detailed for a disgusting duty. These are all in the wings of the eternal stage, set in time. At the centre of the stage is the Master, knowing all these things, kneeling at Peter's dusty feet.

Douglas W. Thompson

O Lord Jesus Christ, suffer us not to stray from thee, who art the Way, nor to distrust thee, who art the Truth, nor to rest in any other thing from thee, who art the Life. Teach us by thy Holy Spirit what to believe, what to do, and wherein to take our rest.

Erasmus

I see his blood upon the rose
And in the stars the glory of his eyes,
His body gleams amid eternal snows,
His tears fall from the skies.

I see his face in every flower;
The thunder and the singing of the birds
Are but his voice – and carven by his power
Rocks are his written word.

All pathways by his feet are worn,
His strong heart stirs the ever-beating sea,
His crown of thorns is twined with every thorn,
His cross is every tree.

Joseph Plunkett

The Christian's great conquest over the world is all contained in the mystery of Christ on the cross. It was there, and from thence, that he taught all Christian how they were to come out of, and conquer, the world, and what they were to do in order to be his disciples.

William Law

There is in fact no theory of the Atonement which is quite as satisfying as the simple statements of the vicarious death of the Christ in the Gospels. This may mean that Faith is able to sense and appropriate an ultimate too deep for human reason.

Reinhold Niebuhr

The cross is the only supreme and sovereign spectacle in all worlds. It is a well of life beneath, in which we can see the face of the heaven above, and the only mirror wherein all things appear in their proper colour.

Thomas Traherne

If this [the good news of Jesus Christ] is dull, then what in heaven's name is worthy to be called exciting? The people who hanged Christ never accused him of being a bore – on the contrary they thought him too dynamic to be safe.

Dorothy L. Sayers

The cross of Christ is the outcome of his deepest mind and of his prayer life. It is more like him than anything else he did. It has in it more of him.

T. R. Glover

Lord Jesus Christ:

>Who in the days of thy flesh
>Didst steadfastly set thy face
>To go to Jerusalem;
>Didst suffer the agony in the garden,
>And dereliction of the cross . . .

>Who yet, for the joy that was set before thee,
>Didst endure the cross,
>Despising the shame,
>And art set down
>At the right hand of God.

Strengthen us,

>When we shrink from unknown ways,
>Hold us firmly when we are afraid;
>Help us to follow thee without swerving
>To the end;
>Out of weakness, make us strong;
>Lighten our darkness,
>And beat down Satan under our feet;
>And finally bring us unto everlasting life.

>Anonymous

>Drop, drop slow tears
>   and bathe those beauteous feet,
>Which brought from heaven
>   the news and Prince of peace:
>Cease not, wet eyes,
>   his mercies to entreat;
>To cry for vengeance
>   sin doth never cease:
>In your deep floods
>   drown all my faults and fears;
>Nor let his eye
>   see sin, but through my tears.

>Phineas Fletcher

What Do You See?

David Parkes

Perhaps you've heard the story of the man who went into a shop and asked, 'Do you sell wasps?'

'Why, no!' was the ready response. 'We're a baker's; can't you see all those lovely cakes?'

'Then why is there a wasp in the window?'

Why indeed! Why did the man see the one wasp rather than the many cakes? And when we look at people, what do we see – their potential sting, or the sweet side of their nature? In prison and in hospital, we are often conditioned to look for the sad and sorry aspects, yet the joyful and even jubilant are there to be found if we but look with open eyes and willing hearts.

There was a man in prison – we'll call him John – who had been convicted many years earlier for murder and was serving a life sentence. He'd almost lost count of the prisons he'd been in as he was moved around the country, a year here, two years there. John had quietened down somewhat and had shown himself to be trustworthy, so he was 'rewarded' by being given employment within the prison. One Friday Peter, another inmate, was told by one of the prison chaplains that his wife had been killed in a road accident. After the chaplain went off duty that evening, John was allowed to be with Peter and share his feelings. Later on, Peter wasn't allowed to go to his wife's funeral and so felt doubly devastated. Once again John came to the rescue and helped Peter to come to terms with the tragedy. Incidentally, Peter was a Buddhist and John would have described himself at that time as an atheist. Some months later John became the chapel orderly, and much later still was baptised and confirmed in the prison chapel with much joy and jubilation. The compassion and care which John showed and his change of heart and mind does not deny in any sense the rightness of the original judgement upon him, but in that place of punishment and deprivation John had become the human face of God; he had identified with Peter's turmoil and lived out Jesus' declaration: 'The Spirit of the Lord is upon me . . . because he has sent me . . . to set at liberty those who are oppressed.'

And oppression is not found only in prisons, it comes unbidden in other places too. Yet circumstances bring unexpected opportunities when God nudges us, if we are but able to be open and willing. In hospital, a very small child had been rushed into the Intensive Care Unit and her family were waiting anxiously for news. The hospital chaplain talked to them and discovered that they had previously asked their local church to christen their daughter, but they had been unwilling to meet the attendance and instruction requirements laid down by the minister. Now their child was very ill. Even as they asked the chaplain if the child could be christened the hospital staff were urgently asking how long he would be, and specialist staff arrived to transfer the child to another hospital. Nonetheless all of them, family and staff, took part in the impromptu christening of the little girl.

In a short time in a hospital, closer contact was made with the family than some church members will allow with their ministers or pastoral workers in years. It's about an acknowledgement of one's own need, an acceptance of one's own vulnerability, and a willingness to allow others to help meet that need and share in that vulnerability. Is that not what Jesus did as he ministered to many? Yet not all were willing to accept him, for they were unable, or did not want to recognise their own need and vulnerability.

There were many times in Jesus' ministry when folk felt that they were quite self-sufficient, and it needed the God-given insight and inspiration of Jesus to reveal their real needs which lay hidden not just to others but to themselves.

An Anglican who described himself firmly as 'high church' came into hospital for a serious operation. While in hospital he had asked for Communion from the duty chaplain who that day happened to be a Free Church minister. Later on, as he went home, he commented, 'Since I've been in hospital I've had time to think about what really matters, and many of the things we think important don't really matter at all.' When looked at through the eyes of Jesus it is shared care and prayer which are important whilst policies, procedures and practices take on a totally different perspective.

There was an inmate in another prison – we'll call him Andrew. He was in prison (again) for drugs and drug-related offences, unable to kick the habit. But after attending an Alpha course in prison, he had come to see his life in a totally different light – the light of the life of Jesus. As Andrew put it, 'Since I've received Jesus into my life I've not touched tobacco or drugs.' That may sound so simple, yet in a prison environment it's anything but, for in the absence of cash both tobacco and drugs become tangible and tempting forms of currency. Andrew's face and life outwardly shone despite the despair and denigration he sometimes felt inside, and he has become an inspiration to others, helping them to remove their moral blindness and recover their insight for what is right and wrong.

For many people to be cured is right and to be incurable is wrong. On this basis a hospice is a place to die and the Macmillan and Marie Curie nurses who visit people's homes help them to prepare for death. Yet those who are privileged to be in a hospice either as a patient or as a member of staff, and those who are fortunate to receive from or work with the Macmillan and Marie Curie service, experience that both are in the business of life and living. Years ago a patient we'll call Lucy had been diagnosed with breast cancer, and had had two operations and radiotherapy. For nearly five years she attended a Macmillan Day Centre where she came to love the care she received and the people she met, for her part giving compassionately to others. After some time she realised that other symptoms were beginning and she sank into the depths of despair. She literally cried out: 'Why me again?' and 'What have I done to deserve this?' She identified so much with those words of Jesus from the cross: 'My God, my God, why have you forsaken me?' for so it seemed God had done to her. Lucy knew that in the midst of Jesus' ministry of healing and wholeness, of love and peace, there was much personal pain and torment. In such circumstances other people can never say, 'I know how you feel!' because they cannot.

For Lucy and for many people in hospitals, hospices, homes and prisons, it is the recognition of Jesus' own problems, his identification with and his empathy for us that means most. Someone once defined empathy as 'your pain in my heart', so family and carers become pain-bearers and hurt-carriers both for the other person and for themselves. But for most (though not all) folk, the time comes when they realise they can do no more, that they are not only in the hands of others but that they are in God's hands, and like Jesus whisper, 'Father, into your hands I commend my Spirit' in total confidence, complete acceptance and full submission.

An old lady, her face full of creases, her body bent with age and infirmity, went to a church service. As people were praying she slumped to the floor, and those around saw her wrinkles disappear, her body straighten and a beautiful smile appear on her lips. When she 'came to' and was asked what had happened, the old lady replied, 'I have seen heaven. And that's where I'm going.' Three weeks later she was diagnosed with terminal cancer, and died after another three weeks. In that time her face regained its wrinkles and her body reverted to its bent posture, but her emotions were untroubled, her spirit was joyful, and those who met her said how great a privilege it was to be with her.

When we look at Jesus, what do we see? For many people in prison, both inmates and officers, and for those in hospital, both patients and staff, it is his humanity – his life lived amidst the trials and temptations of his own society, his identification with our pleasures and our pains, our joys and our sorrows – that rings true, bringing consolation, comfort and courage. His life personifies God's love for us, and exemplifies our love for God in response. It is only a few, a favoured few, who are privileged to look beyond the life that is and glimpse the glory of the divine Jesus with the promise of the life that is to be. For the remainder of us, faith and trust in him and not sense and sight of him must suffice.

Autumn Allegory

Prue Phillipson

It is autumn as I write and some of my grandchildren are collecting conkers. The shiny red-brown nuts are easy to spot among the fallen leaves but they are less distinguishable if they are still in their spiky, dull green shells. The finder must have sharp eyes and then take the trouble to break them open to get at the treasure within, sealed in its inner coating. The children stroke this with their fingers and exclaim at how soft and cosy it feels.

The little scene makes me think of the human condition, our nature in which Jesus lived and died and rose again for our redemption. It is so easy for us to want to inhabit a safe shell like the conker. Most of us, in the affluent, developed world, sit comfortably cocooned in our daily routines for weeks or months at a time, taking for granted our sufficiency of food, clothing and well-equipped homes. Even if we profess to be committed Christians and have our times of daily prayer and corporate worship, we are in our warm familiar setting and shielded from hurt and suffering. Sadly we can become inured to the tragedies of others by a surfeit of television images. We are sympathetic and ready to give some aid, but we are inured because we can switch it all off, literally, and remain in our comfortable shell.

But how different was Jesus when he lived his life upon this earth! He was Son of God and Son of Man, Lord of all things and a humble boy growing in devout faith to manhood in a carpenter's household. But this was no cocooned existence. From the little we are told of his life we know that he must have fought off the temptations that beset the young, that he was earnest in studying the Scriptures and was open to the call of God his Father. When he knew the time had come to prepare for his ministry he went into the wilderness, willingly submitting his body to a severe physical trial and then, when he was at his lowest ebb, facing spiritual temptation. How his natural will must have longed for a cocoon into which to creep not only from night cold, noontide heat, hunger and thirst, but from the encounter with the powers of darkness that dared to dangle before his mind's eye all that ministering angels could do for him if he chose to summon them! But he knew that hiding away was not his destiny; it would not achieve God's purpose of salvation for humankind, in which sacrificial love was to conquer evil in all its forms. He drew no shell around him but the strength of the Holy Spirit, and it was the devil who slunk away defeated.

When he embarked on his ministry other sufferings were added to his daily experience – weary journeys, storms, homelessness, the clamour of crowds – but far worse must have been the spiritual suffering: grief at the pain and isolation of others – lepers, blind beggars, cripples – which he (unlike us) truly shared, his heart burning with love and his soul uplifted in prayer. And can we ever imagine the sorrow he must have felt at the cruelty of humankind? He saw brutal punishments, floggings and stonings. Did he witness a crucifixion before his own? They were not uncommon. His agony in the Garden of Gethsemane encompassed not only the physical suffering he knew he had to face but the spiritual darkness of taking the burden of our sins, the horror of which he could feel looming over him. And that burden included so much more than crude, ugly sins. His soul abhorred the smug hypocrisy of the religious élite. He couldn't reach them through the shell of their pride and complacency. Even among his disciples he had to rebuke vainglory and emulation. He must have felt deeply their fall from the heights to which he was trying to lift them. Truly there was no shell for him to hide in. No wonder he yearned to draw aside into the silence and seek strength from God.

What can we learn from him in this? We can never enter fully into his suffering but we know he shares ours – our tough learning periods of long, drawn-out trials which break through our shells and rip them from us, leaving us raw and exposed. At such times, when daily life is neither easy nor predictable, he is there, a rock to cling to, a fountain of love to sustain us.

In between there are blessèd periods of quiet and these should be spent close to God, as Jesus spent his quiet times. Yet so often they become shell-building times when we are tempted into faults we don't even recognise as such: impatience, dishonest excuses, self-deception, irritation at disruptions to our comfort, like a phone call when we are settling down to watch television. These are not trials in which we think of seeking God's help. We don't see our reactions as sins. They are natural, soon over, and doesn't everybody behave like that? They are the world's attitudes, prickly and soon forming a hard shell like the horse chestnut's. We hear on every side, 'Don't lie down under that'; 'Stick up for your rights'; 'Give as good as you get'; 'No one expects you to put yourself out like that'; 'It's time you started thinking of yourself.' So we snuggle down again, comfortably smothering our weak pricks of conscience.

But this is not Jesus' teaching. There are no half-measures in his Sermon on the Mount. It is not enough to love our friends, we must love our enemies as well. It is not enough to avoid the big sins like murder or adultery, we must keep our hearts free from hatred and lust. Matthew 5 ends with the shattering verse: 'Be perfect, therefore, even as your heavenly Father is perfect.' In the parable of the lord and the stewards (Luke 12:48) Jesus shows that his expectations are greatest from his own disciples, who should be on the watch and active in his service. And he

130

warns us, 'How hard it will be for those who have wealth to enter the kingdom of God!' (Mark 10:23). Most of the time we don't think of ourselves as rich, but when we are suffering, from whatever cause – illness, bereavement, war, fire or flood – we see that in our cocooned years we were rich indeed. But because at such times we have more to lose we tend to be less ready then to meet the demands of his service.

In the autumn wood I dwell on the ease and sweetness of my present daily life as I walk with my husband and grandchildren. The colours are rich and glorious in the low afternoon sunlight. It is one of those moments of pure joy and thankfulness, but it also alerts me to the need for more intense prayer when I realise I may again have been shell-building.

Even writing, like any human employment which we enjoy, can become a shell in itself. It was not until I had been through my hardest testing times, including long-time caring and bereavement, that I began to realise God might be expecting me to express my faith more specifically through my writing and – harder still – might be expecting me to try more persistently to be published. Sending off manuscripts is in itself a shell-piercing experience, but coming to terms with rejection is even more so. When a breakthrough finally happens there is the accompanying sense of personal exposure – has one's writing been for the glory of God or one's own ego? And all the time there is a sort of longing to draw a comfortable, protective shell of daily living around one, doing the easier things one enjoys and trying to escape God's purpose, whatever it may be.

There is nothing at all wrong with the gentler periods of life. I am certainly grateful for them when they come, but relief after a great trial need not mean that we stop meeting each new day as a challenge to spread the love of God within our immediate domestic sphere. No horizon is too limited – of space or time. And when we are full of his love that is the most shell-piercing tool of all.

So as I look at this autumn scene I hope that God the gatherer finds many souls shining like conkers – and how I long to be of that number! – for he may grieve over many more green spiked shells inside whose soft cushions there are bright souls snugly bedded, but sadly not yet ripe for his service.

When Jesus came to Galilee,
 By stony ways he trod –
Jesus, who came for you and me,
 To bring us home to God.

And when he hung on Calvary,
 The door was opened wide;
Bitter his pains, but you and I
 Have life because he died.

So dear the love, so great the price
 He paid, and shall there be
No answering love and sacrifice
 For him from you and me?

       Anonymous

He became poor that we through his poverty might be rich. He took the form of a servant that we might obtain our freedom. He descended that we might be exalted. He was tempted that we might conquer. He was dishonoured that he might dignify us. He died that he might save us.

       Gregory Nazianzen

O, you who weep, come to him who weeps too;
O, you who suffer, come to him who cures;
O, you who fear, here he smiles on you;
O, you who die, come to him who endures.

       Victor Hugo

No word he said. Nothing.
They had plenty to say.

He, who for love's sake being Man,
Stood, for love's sake, condemned –
And said no word of blame, no word of warm defence:
Nothing – until
At last, hung high on the crucifixion hill
He made his retort to their taunts and lies,
Their proud, pitiful triumph;
Gave them his answer: 'Father, forgive them,
They know not what they do.'

Anonymous

The path of Jesus which leads to a fuller and richer life passes through a sort of death; in Jesus' own case, a literal death, on a cross at Calvary. In the case of Christians, who must take up a cross if they truly wish to follow Jesus, his way to life is *via* self-giving; it is by letting go our self-centredness, our defensiveness, our fear, our insecurity, and instead, by embracing – with courage, but knowing the risk – an alternative way of humble service, of costly loving, of living without power and without status in society.

David Deeks

What a transformation . . . when our gaze is steadily fixed on the Lamb of God. Then harmony, not violence, fills the heart; then gentleness, not cruelty, guides our hand; love, not hate, binds people together. If we are to overcome the evil that rages in our own souls and torments the earth we must see and follow the Lamb of God. If ever we are to know the wonderful love of the Father, we must gaze on the face of the Crucified, who takes away the sin of the world and leads us back to God.

Leslie Davison

I said:
'Lord, I cannot bear it,
This constant pain – this constant suffering.
Help me – save me – deliver me;
O heal these wounds!'
He said, 'Be still – be calm – listen for my voice.'
I fell into silence,
And in dark waters I waited for him to speak,
To say: 'I will heal these wounds,
I will heal these wounds,
I will take them from thee.'
I waited – time stood still,
Then, all at once, he spoke:
And oh – he said:
'My heart is wounded, too.'

Anonymous

Nothing in the world has ever been so completely lost as was Christianity at the time that Christ was crucified. And in the understanding of the moment, never in the world has anyone accomplished so little by the sacrifice of a consecrated life as did Jesus Christ. And yet in this same instant, eternally understood, he had accomplished all.

Sören Kierkegaard

My mind is for ever splintered
on the anvil of Time
and my spirit wanders restlessly
through the caverns of Eternity.
You ask me why?
I was an ordinary legionary in Jerusalem
nigh two thousand years ago.
One chill, windy morning
we nailed a Man to a cross.
(It was a routine job.)
He died rather soon.
I remember throwing down the dice
(we were gambling for his clothes),
and, picking up my spear, a trusty weapon
that had seen me through many a skirmish
In Gaul, and Libya,
I thrust it into his side, to make certain before telling the
      centurion.
I saw blood and water trickle down the haft
gripped in my hands,
I saw more – though, by the bird of Jupiter,
I wish I hadn't.
Looking into his deathless eyes
I saw his heart broken
for me.

Chandran Devansen

The Challenge of Jesus

Daleep Mukarji

As I write this we have been celebrating the jubilee of 2000 years since Christ's birth. There has been much hype about the events, the fireworks, the parties and the fears about the Y2K bug, from the UK right across the world. We have also had some analysis of recent events, attempts to review history and predict the future. Various lists have been prepared. We have been invited to choose the person of the century – or of the millennium. Sadly, one sees very little reference to Jesus. Surely he is the person at the centre of all this? We need to consider who this person Jesus is, and what influence he may have had or has in the world today.

For people like me, born and brought up in the South – the developing world – Jesus was initially someone brought to us along with colonial powers. We saw a Western Jesus – blue-eyed, blond and fair-skinned. Sadly some colonisation went with 'Christian-isation'. The new powers wanted to 'civilise', and this meant westernise and modernise with often little regard for race, creed or culture.

Today there is a rejection of this approach as Christians in the South are trying to understand more about the person of Jesus in their own cultures and contexts. Suddenly they are more able to identify with him. He too was born in a colonial context: to a working class family, in a slum area of Bethlehem; his parents fled as refugees to Eygpt.

This Jesus was one of them, and one of us too – from the South – and poor. He spoke of his mission to bring good news to the poor, to proclaim release to the captives, and to set free the oppressed. He preached the kingdom of God, speaking of a new understanding of relationships with essential values of justice, respect, dignity and love. He was young, too – just thirty-three when he died. Radical, revolutionary, a role model well worth following.

It was this aspect of the humanity, character and message of Jesus that has inspired liberation theologians over the years to raise questions about the society in which we all live, and to question the poverty and disparity of it. This same message has provided hope for women, dalits (belonging to the outcast society), indigenous peoples and freedom fighters from across the globe, as they have sought to build this new world community. Jesus' message is still a challenge for us today, as we see many around us denied life, dignity, rights and in many other ways dehumanised. In the context of a world where so many are broken, oppressed, marginalised, made poor and suffering, Jesus' message remains full of hope, new life and energy. It is essentially good news.

Followers of Christ in his time on earth were invited and challenged to follow him in actions which restored fullness of life – to stand in solidarity with others. For us today, this challenge inspires us to participate in our world too, to take our places in the struggles for justice and to stand up against the structures, systems and forces that have exploited and oppressed people. And so our calling, in keeping with God's mission, through the person of Jesus, is to build a new world community where all are valued as children of the living God, and where all can have the fullness of life.

It is this very dimension of Jesus that has attracted me personally. It provides the framework for my life and work, from a medical and health background back home, to the World Council of Churches, and now, since 1998, with Christian Aid.

It is estimated that one billion people live today in abject poverty, a truly shocking figure. In recent years we have seen a commitment to reduce the number of people on our earth who live in poverty by half by the year 2015. But is this target possible? Will it be achieved? In sub-Saharan Africa alone 19,000 children die every day because of the debt burdens of their country. Repayments to the Western world mean that little gets spent on health, education, development, and so the list goes on.

The jubilee Jesus proclaimed was one of good news to the poor. It was about debt relief, the protection of the land and environment, help for the poor – and Jesus sent his followers out to preach this. I believe it is critical that we too must follow this charge. We must see it as central to the Gospel message, and be out in the world living up to it. Over the centuries many Christians have done just this and provided the necessary challenges and inspiration for others. Our response to the challenge may not only change us, but more importantly it may help to change the world!

Working in rural south India in the early 1980s in a Christian Aid supported programme, I was involved in community health and rural development activities. At that time women were often given very low wages, abused at home and ignored in society, because of socio-cultural factors. We facilitated women's adult education, the formation of social groups (mahila mandals) and enabled the setting up of self-help co-operatives with small bank loans for economic development. We saw dalit women gain a sense of dignity, self-esteem and self-reliance. They were changed themselves, and went on to become key agents of change in their families and villages.

Surely this was a reflection of God within the community, where the creative power of Christ liberates and empowers, and gives life. It is a message of the affirmation of people's humanity in a world in which everyone is a child of God and made in his image – irrespective of gender, caste, status, religion or colour. We can make a difference. Jesus did – and he continues to do so and call people to be his agents of change in the world today. We share this message of faith in a Jesus who cares because he was one of us. Thus I believe that faith becomes a source of energy and courage, for the transformation of community – into a new earth in the perspective of the reign of God.

The great principle of our relationship with Jesus Christ is abundantly clear: he became like us, that we might become like him. He became a person, like us, lived our life and died our death, in order that we might become perfect like him and rise like him out of death into life for evermore.

S. B. Frost

Jesus . . . the pain-bearer bears our separations, our forsakenness, our grief, our loneliness in his own body 'on the tree'. He bears the sins of the whole world. In this sense he is the scapegoat. Just as the goat is sent running to escape into the wilderness carrying the sins of the people, so Jesus takes our desert-pain into his own wilderness. He suffers on our behalf and in so doing feels the separation and alienation caused by our self-centredness.

Martin Eggleton

His enemies had done all they could do. We see him in the hands of those who loved him. Two of them are here, Joseph and Nicodemus. In that supreme hour Joseph did the thing of ultimate courage. He went straight to Pilate and begged the body of Jesus. Then we see those two men acting together. The sepulchre was rock-hewn; it was in a garden, near the place where they crucified him. It was Joseph's tomb. There they brought the body of Jesus, and there we see these two men wrapping it round, with a hundred pounds of spices intermixed with the wrappings. Never let us forget that when Peter, and the rest of the crowd with him had all run away, two secret disciples took care of the dead body of Jesus, and buried it with love.

G. Campbell Morgan

The crucifixion of Jesus did not turn out to be the end of Jesus. The one whom the disciples had followed was still 'ahead' of them. Death had not left him behind. Even after his death he was still present with him. So God himself had done a new and wonderful thing. He had brought Jesus from the dead. Faith in the risen Christ is at the heart of the Christian proclamation. The 'mechanics' of the resurrection are matters of dispute. The precise meaning of the 'resurrection' remains elusive. Nevertheless, that which escapes comprehension can be communicated to love and obedience.

Peter Baelz

I know that in Christ, by the power of the Holy Spirit, I can learn to die to all that would isolate me from God and my fellow men, that I may live the new life centred on Christ and shared with his and my brothers and sisters, a life which through the resurrection transcends my mortality and gives it eternal significance.

Graham Leonard

Christ has illuminated the world, not by what he did, but by what he was. They tell me that the Easter morning has revealed his glory; rather would I say that his glory has revealed the Easter morning. It is not resurrection that has made Christ; it is Christ that has made resurrection.

George Matheson

'Tis the spring of souls today;
Christ hath burst his prison,
And from three days' sleep in death
As the sun hath risen;
All the winter of our sins,
Long and dark, is flying
From his light, to whom we give
Laud and praise undying.

St John of Damascus, tr. J. M. Neale

Sometimes when I am far out at sea I know the sun is risen by the light reflected from my cottage windows. I know Christ is risen by his light reflected in the faces of some of my fellows, and the light of his glory in my own life.

A Cornish fisherman

Christ is risen,
and the angels rejoice.
Christ is risen and life reigns in freedom.
Christ is risen, and there is none left dead in the tomb.
For Christ, being raised from the dead, has become the first-fruits
of those that slept. To him be glory and dominion to the ages of
ages.

St John Chrysostom

May the glad dawn
    Of Easter morn
Bring holy joy to thee!

May the calm eve
    Of Easter leave
A peace divine with thee!

May Easter Day
    To thine heart say,
'Christ died and rose for thee.'

May Easter night
    On thine heart write,
'O Christ, I live to thee!'

Anonymous

I walked across the common in the bright, sunny, quite empty morning, listening to the rising of the lark as he went up in an ecstasy of song into the blue unclouded sky and gave in his Easter morning hymn at Heaven's Gate. Then came the echo and answer of earth as the Easter bells rang out their joy peals from the church towers all round. It was very sweet and lovely, the bright silent sunny morning, and the lark rising and singing alone in the blue sky, and suddenly the morning air all alive with music of sweet bells ringing for the joy of the resurrection. 'The Lord is risen', smiled the sun, 'The Lord is risen', sang the lark. And the church bells in their joyous pealing answered from tower to tower: 'He is risen indeed!'

Francis Kilvert

Jesus and Some Modern Thinkers

Gordon Wakefield

From the New Testament onwards there have been hundreds of writings about Jesus Christ and his position both in world history and Christian doctrine. I want to look at the work of three writers of the second half of the twentieth century and at one very recent study. The writers are technical theologians, but I shall deal with them as simply as possible to help us to shed light on the mystery of who Jesus is.

In 1948 there was published *God was in Christ*[1] by Donald M. Baillie of the Church of Scotland. It had great influence chiefly because it interpreted Jesus in terms of 'the paradox of grace'. If Paul could say of any good that he was or did, 'Not I but the grace of God that is within me', could not Jesus say this perfectly? He was all of grace, totally possessed by the self-giving love of God, which we see intermittently in the saints. This solves the problem of how he could at once be God and man, Divine and human. The grace is altogether of God and yet a human quality revealed in words and deeds. Baillie says it 'will enable us to combine the most transcendent claims of a full and high Christology with the frankest recognition of the humanity of the historical Jesus'.

This has been criticised as insufficiently stressing the absolute uniqueness of the Incarnation and being too concerned with its psychological effects. But it was found amazingly enlightening by many.

Two years later, in 1950, W. R. Matthews published the Maurice Lectures he had given in the University of London entitled *The Problem of Christ in the Twentieth Century*.[2] Matthews was Dean of St Paul's, an office he was to hold for a further eighteen years. He became a dear friend of mine in his old age, gentle, affectionate, ecumenical. He was essentially a philosopher of religion and a fine and lucid one. His book on Christ is thoroughly orthodox. He affirms the Incarnation, that God became man in Jesus Christ, unequivocally, ('the Son "came down from heaven" – from the eternal into time') but he does not think that the classic explanations of the early Fathers and the Creeds, though inevitable in their time, are adequate for our time.

He feels that the Early Fathers' understanding of Jesus Christ was defective in four ways. Firstly they had no adequate concept of personality, secondly they describe God as a self-sufficient being, thirdly they assert that Christ had two natures, Divine and human, and therefore two wills, and fourthly the word 'nature' is inapplicable to God, for it implies that there is a class of beings who share Divine qualities.

Matthews examines the Incarnation in the light of modern psychology and in particular in terms of the unconscious. Was the 'libido' ie 'a subterranean stream which is, in a general and vague way sexual, and from which is derived the motive force of the personality' present in Christ? It could be so, provided the libido is not related to original sin from which Jesus was free.

Matthews suggests that telepathy raised to the highest degree may explain the belief that Christ bore the sins of the world. He repudiates the theory of penal substitution but imagines a case where 'all the barriers of the self are down and all the thoughts, emotions and desires of all the world flow in – the muddy stream of all human mental life'. The conscious self knows them all from within but is not overcome by them. 'Would not such an experience be bearing the sins of many and the victory over them?' But

Matthews does not accept that psychology 'can give the final answer to any of the fundamental questions'.

His conclusion uses the concepts of 'pattern' and 'inspiration'. The Incarnation may be regarded as an identity of patterns between the Divine will and the human will, while the union of Divine and human in Christ may be explained in terms of inspiration. Jesus, more than the saints who are partially and fitfully inspired, was wholly and continuously inspired by the Spirit of God.

Not many would feel that Matthews' tentative solutions to the problem of Christ are fully satisfying. But they raise important questions and are insightful in their answers. And he was insistent against the theologian Rudolf Bultmann that the records are sufficient for us to know the Jesus of history, the details of his words and work. Also he emphasises in his sermons that belief in the resurrection is a Gospel. 'It is not a belief that some anonymous individual has risen but that the Son of Man has overcome death and dies no more.' And elsewhere he writes:

> The personal and individual relation with the Saviour is inescapable in the New Testament and in Christian experience ever since. 'He loved me and gave himself up for me,' says St Paul and we can hear the wonder and the gratitude in those simple words. They are at the heart of the Gospel.

Much more recently, Maurice Wiles, Regius Professor Emeritus of Divinity in the University of Oxford, has written of Jesus, and many would suspect his orthodoxy. He believes that in theology as in other forms of knowledge there is no finality but that there must be a continued searching and openness. He has not Matthews' belief in the Incarnation as the foundation of our understanding of Jesus Christ.

He does not believe that this doctrine is required for it to be true that the world depends for its very existence on a God who cares about human suffering, who has a purpose for the world which men can come in part at least to know, and who elicits from men a mature response of faith and love in which sin can be overcome and the goals of human life begin to be realised. Moreover, the central figure within history in whom the recognition and realisation of these things is focused is Jesus Christ.

Recently, in *Reason to Believe*,[3] Wiles has written about Jesus. In the four Gospels it is hard to distinguish between what goes back to Jesus himself and the evangelists' adaptation since 'their aim was to present the traditions about Jesus which were known to them in the form appropriate to the situation of those for whom they were writing'. So Matthew and Luke who both used Mark felt free to alter what Mark had written. But this does not undermine the Gospels and the life of Jesus for Christian faith.

For as we seek to interpret them in our own contemporary context, our reflections on the records of Jesus and the religious uses to which those records were put can contribute to the building up of our own Christian vision of the world.

Jesus called God 'Father' and his sense of God's presence and its overriding claim on him was sustained by a life of prayer which entailed struggle and suffering to the last. And his proclamation of the kingdom, the ruling power of God and the possibility of living in obedience to it was sustained both by his parables which demanded 'ears to hear', and the imagination of his hearers to apply the stories to their own lives; and his works of healing which imply what life in the kingdom is like and the power of faith to transform human beings to make it possible. And he made friendships with those relegated to the margins of society. He was 'numbered with the transgressors' in his death because he had been in his life. The doctrine of the Incarnation 'symbolises the intimacy of God's involvement with the world'.

So from different standpoints these three thinkers interpret Jesus, Son of God and Son of Man. In the early months of 2000, Geza Vermes' *The Changing Faces of Jesus*[4] was published. He describes the different view of Jesus in the New Testament itself beginning with the Fourth Gospel's assertion that Jesus is the Word or Mind of God made flesh. He goes on to Paul's concentration on Jesus as the Saviour from sin who makes us right with God, rather than on his earthly life. Then follows the first three Gospels' account of his ministry, adapted to the preaching of the Gospel beyond its original home. Vermes, a Jew, is anxious to concentrate on the Jewishness of Jesus, which is fair.

I do not find any of this disturbing. The fact remains that this man and his, in some ways, tragic story possessed the minds of his followers long after his shameful death and was a 'real presence' in their lives. I believe – differing here somewhat from Wiles – that the affirmations of the creeds, though in the categories of their own time, are an authentic development from the Jesus of history. He is the second person of a God in three persons or aspects of being, whom we approach through him.

1   D. M. Baillie, *God was in Christ*, Faber & Faber, 1948.
2   W. R. Matthews, Maurice Lectures: *The Problem of Christ in the Twentieth Century*, OUP, 1950.
3   Maurice Wiles, *The Remaking of Christian Doctrine*, SCM Press, 1974; *Faith and the Mystery of God*, SCM Press, 1982; *Reason to Believe*, SCM Press, 1999.
4   Geza Vermes, *The Changing Faces of Jesus*, Allen Lane, The Penguin Press, 2000.

'And he went in to tarry with them.' Jesus did not come to those two disciples [on the road to Emmaus] that day because he must give them a theological message which the apostles were too emotionally upset to understand just then. He came to them as he came to Mary and to Peter, because he was the Good Shepherd who must go on caring for the sheep, and because these two had strayed the farthest along the road from where the flock was gathered.

Gordon Rupp

Jesus is not dead. He is alive today – to the issues of the present situation, alive to the special human problems of this generation, alive to guide us, if we will allow him, through the moral mazes of our time by his own indwelling presence.

Ian Macpherson

The disciples at Emmaus, we are told, knew him in the breaking of bread. It is the symbol of hospitality, of friendship. And we, if we are to live consciously in his companionship, must give him the marks of our friendship in our turn. Now I call you not servants but friends, he explicitly told his disciples; we have only to do our part . . . not just a sharing of superficialities such as exists between acquaintances, but a sharing of the deep things of life, the deep thoughts and ambitions, the secrets of the heart. Our Lord, for his part, calls us not servants but friends, because, he says, he has made known to us the secrets of his own heart, has shown us the plot of his own love story: it only remains for us to do the same.

Gerald Vann

Several hundred people were so sure that they had seen him after he had risen (1 Corinthians 15:6) that the belief was the centre and moving power of their lives. If you grip this truth and make it the centre of your lives, you may leave all questions of doctrines etc, as open questions. Just be always reminding yourselves, 'But I know that Jesus rose and lives.'

Dr Hely Almond

All God asks you to do [is to] believe the record he has given concerning Jesus; put your heart's trust in him. You may be assured that you have life eternal for 'he that hath the Son hath life; and he that hath not the Son hath not life. These things have I written unto you that believe on the name of the Son of God; that ye may *know* – not merely hope, not just have a reasonable assurance, but full assurance – that ye *have* eternal life.'

H. A. Ironside

Love is the key of life and death,
Of hidden, heavenly harmony:
As three times to his saint he saith,
He saith to me, he saith to thee,
Breathing his grace-conferring breath,
'Lovest thou me?'

O Lord, I have such feeble faith,
Such feeble hope to comfort me;
But love it is, is strong as death,
And I love thee.

Christina Rossetti

The truth about Jesus Christ moves beyond simplicity; its mystery continues to humiliate us in our attempts to tie down this man, this God, in words which cannot stay uncorrupted by moth and rust. It is true that the man from Nazareth who *was* the Christ *is* alive today, is our contemporary; he *was* God for us, he *is* God for us. Yet he continues to challenge us to find him out, to rediscover him again and again in the complexities and simplicities of the life he calls us to live.

John Beer

Before Christ left the world he had kindled a light which would never go out. The courage of a life that was ready to go to any length of sacrifice and the constancy of a faith that would be true to God and to himself at all costs – though it meant his death on a cross – would in the end draw all men unto him.

John H. Litten

What do we make of the story of Jesus? It is not a comfortable or an easy story. It is harrowing and tragic in parts. It is challenging and demanding. It shakes our foundations. What do we make of Jesus of Nazareth, controversial as he was? . . . I find his story demanding but compelling, that his teaching makes sense, and that his death and resurrection are for me pointers to the heart of God and the meaning of life. In him I catch a glimpse of God, and see a way of living that is real. I believe in this story. I want to be a follower too.

Stephen Dawes

It must have happened in later years
That Peter,
Mary,
Thomas,
Those who had been his friends
Would walk along the road where they had
been with him
And say to their companions,
'This is where he healed the lepers –
There were ten, you know,
And only one came back to thank him.
We were standing there beside that tree.'
Or, 'This is where he took the children
In his arms
And blessed them.
He was sitting on that rock.'

Familiar places must have held
Such memories of him,
Almost as though he still were there
And they could hear his voice.

So memories persist,
And we recall our meeting with the Master,
'I was here
When first I felt his living presence.
Knew within my deepest heart
He was my Saviour, too.'
Or, 'There his healing came to me.'
Or, 'Yonder is the place where first
My prayer became companionship with him.'

James Asa Johnson

Jesus Christ: The Fruition of God's Purpose

Donald Hilton

'Follow me!' the man said, and they left their nets and homes, their counting desks and their security, and followed him. Had you asked them who they were following they would have had their ready answers. He was a good man; that much was obvious from the way he treated people. A teacher, too; they'd already listened in wide-eyed amazement at the way ancient truth sprang from his lips as though it had been newly-minted that very morning. This rabbi had a new message that did no disservice to all they had learned in the synagogue. And a friend, also; even in the earliest days it seemed right to think of him in such a way.

It's experience that tells you how to describe people. Experience comes before the label – and if later experience doesn't fit your first description, you change the description to match the new experience.

The revolutionary politician who, once in office, becomes complacent and adopts bland policies will soon find people describing him in a different way. The newly-appointed teacher so full of new ideas that she's called 'a breath of fresh air' soon gets a different title if experience shows that those new ideas quickly wither as she follows a static teaching programme. And the other way round: the new manager who first seemed so indecisive can later reveal a steely determination. We can misread the qualities of a leader and be forced, by later experience, to change the way we describe him or her.

The disciples had frequently to rethink the nature and purpose of the man whose word of challenge first came to them on the seashore. Their labels soon wore out. This 'good man' remained good but they realised that there was much more to be said about him than that. This 'rabbi' was seen in a new light; his teaching had an unexpected sharp edge to it that frustrated and angered the Pharisees but delighted the crowds. Traditional rabbis spoke from books; this teacher spoke from life and quickly broke out of the narrow confines of the 'rabbi' label. Jesus ever remained a leader but the kind of leader they had never met before. What leader washed his followers' feet? Then there was the way he talked about God, as though God was not only with him, but within him. Or was it that he was within God?

Their experience of this man was so deep and comprehensive that it became indefinable. He eluded full description. Whatever they said about him seemed inadequate. They had to pile title on title to get anywhere near describing their experience of this complete and comprehensive man. Just who was he?

One day, Jesus began to tease out their ideas about him. He asked what other people were saying. 'Some say you are John the Baptist,' they replied, 'others Elijah, Jeremiah or one of the prophets.' They were all good answers. Jesus did have something of the ascetic nature of John, and something of the 'stand up and be counted' mentality of Elijah who had confronted the false prophets of Baal. Jesus' teaching often resonated with Jeremiah's prophecy of a new law which would be 'written in the heart' rather than on tablets of stone. He was all these things but so much more.

Jesus' question became more pointed. 'Who do *you* say I am?' he asked. 'Our friend,' they might once simply have said. It was still true, but there was so much more to be said. 'A leader of people' could have come to their lips. But qualities of leadership had emerged which they had never known before. A healer he certainly was. All were true but none were true enough; he was all these and more. Peter pushed the description further – probably as far as anyone could go in Jesus' lifetime. He blurted out their growing conviction: 'You are the Messiah, the Son of the living God.'

Had they known it, a later hymn writer would struggle in the same way:

> Join all the glorious names
> of wisdom, love and power,
> that ever mortals knew,
> that angels ever bore;
> All are too mean to speak his worth,
> too mean to set my Saviour forth.

> Isaac Watts

Then came Calvary followed by Easter, and crowned by Pentecost. It was much later that those disciples first wrestled with the greater dilemma which has perplexed theologians ever since. They had known this man, walked with him, shared meals and parties with him, heard him laugh, knew that he enjoyed company and yet sometimes wanted to be alone. They had savoured his human confidence and also watched him cry out for help in mortal agony. His flesh was like their flesh. Prick him and he bled. In bereavement, he wept. Blood like theirs flowed through his veins. Beyond question he was a man.

Yet what man had ever lived beyond death and met his disciples beyond the grave as though death itself had died? What man could take human suffering in its depths and redeem it? With what other man could you feel that you were walking with God, intimately? Their very experience made them assert the seeming impossible: this 'man' is God; this 'God' is man.

An anonymous fifteenth century writer pondered these irreconcilable opposites and decided that, since experience had proved both to be true, the Christian faith had touched profound mystery:

> A God and yet a man?
> A maid and yet a mother?
> Wit wonders how wit can
> Conceive this or the other.
>
> God, Truth itself, doth teach it.
> Man's wit sinks too far under
> By reason's power to reach it:
> Believe, and leave to wonder.

In the city of Nicaea in 325 AD, theologians embodied the mystery in a creed. Jesus is: the only Son of God, eternally begotten of the Father, God from God, Light from Light, true God from true God, begotten not made, of one Being with the Father, through him all things were made.

If one side of a see-saw goes up, the other must come down. That's the danger in the God/man description of Jesus. If you stress the divinity of Jesus you minimise his humanity and rob him of his common touch. If you stress his humanity you anchor him to the ground and deny his uplifting power to save.

Use the idea of a circle to understand Jesus and the same problem emerges. Put the humanity of Jesus at the centre of the circle of Christian conviction and his divinity is pushed to the circumference edge where it might be lost; put his divinity at the centre and he is no longer the man of the people the four Gospels clearly reveal.

Perhaps an ellipse is a better model. A circle has one focus with an equidistant circumference; an ellipse has two foci with a circumference varying in distance from each of them. If divinity is seen as one focus and humanity as the other they are no longer irreconcilable opposites but act together to allow our faith to live creatively on the circumference.

Those early disciples, seeking to know the nature of this man they had decided to follow, were content to live simultaneously with many descriptions: friend, teacher, healer, rabbi, servant, lord. No one name was enough but together they reached a climax of meaning.

There is another way of looking at it. Suppose that God's true intention is that humanity should reach a height far beyond anything we know at the moment. Suppose further, that just as the rest of creation has evolved from the lesser to the greater, so our present human nature is just one stage towards what humanity will eventually become. And suppose that in the ultimate development of human nature, through a process like evolution, the final goal will be the closest possible intimacy with God. Could it be that Jesus was the firm evidence of that process and goal? Is humanity on a journey in which what we now call 'human' is only a stage on the way, and was Jesus the first truly authentic human being to emerge?

Instead of see-saws, circles and ellipses, a French theologian and scientist, Pierre Teilhard de Chardin (1881-1955), used evolution as a model to understand the Christian faith. It might lead us to imagine that if into primitive plant life God planted the possibility of the evolution of a complicated structure such as an orchid or rose, and if into the simple biological structure of the amoeba God planted the possibility of the complex structures that produced the animal and human kingdoms, could God also have planted into the evolutionary process not only the humanity we know ourselves but also the perfect humanity represented by Christ? Is Jesus the end point in the evolutionary process, the symbol and precursor of all that God intended us to be? It's an idea that breaks through the usual contradictions of a man/God and sees Jesus as the fulfilment of all that God intended humanity to become.

We are now well into the third millennium celebrating Jesus Christ, the same yesterday, today and forever. Does his constancy lie in the fact that he is a sign and foretaste of God's ultimate purpose; a destiny towards which all those who love and serve him are being drawn, and to which God will eventually lead all creation?

For the faith of the disciples the resurrection of Jesus became the most fixed and incontrovertible certainty . . . their faithfulness in the presence of the death of Jesus was changed into their conviction of his resurrection; [it] became to their consciousness a matter of fact, and possessed for them all the reality of historical fact.

Ferdinand Baur

At first sight it seems strange that the early Christians – Jews who believed so utterly in the *one* God – should ever have ascribed divinity to a man living among men. Their affirmation of Jesus' lordship could never have been made unless, as a matter of personal experience, they had felt that in Jesus they had met One whose influence upon them and their fellow-believers was without parallel in human experience, and that the divine events which had centred in the person and work of Jesus had changed the whole status and prospects of humankind.

Alfred H. S. Pask

'A cloud received him out of their *sight'*, but perhaps [the disciples] were already beginning to know that out of their *reach* he would never be. During forty days they had been given glimpses of his risen presence, and gradually they were learning that what was true for them in those great hours must always be true . . . The risen Lord would always be there; it was only a cloud that veiled him from their sight. Behind the cloud he would be with them all the days.

Francis B. James

It gives us pause to see [Jesus] standing back to give room and time for the seed to grow, and to hear him speak of the earth bringing forth fruit of itself, the sower 'knows not how'. There is such faith and humility in that word as might well bring tears to our eyes. He knew, indeed, that he was not leaving the seed alone. He was leaving it to a thousand ministries . . . to the Spirit who never leaves us, and the Love that will not let us go. The most sensitive and vulnerable heart that ever beat on earth was also the most serene. That is the miracle of Jesus.

J. Jeremias

By his Ascension our Lord did the very opposite of what the disciples thought he did. No more was he distant from them, compelled by time and space to be here and there, but for ever 'nearer than breathing, closer than hands and feet'. So the Lord went away for a time that he might be near them for ever. The Ascension our Lord himself declared to be expedient for his disciples, because it would bring him nearer to them in his *alter ego*, the Comforter. Through him, the Spirit of truth, he became the strengthener and guide of those men he loved, whom he would never leave as orphans but to whom he said: 'Lo, I am with you always, even unto the end of the world.'

J. Ernest Rattenbury

I swear I will never henceforth have to do
with the faith that tells the best!
I will have to do only with that faith that
leaves the best untold.

Walt Whitman

The Jews wail for their king to come, and he does come, riding on an ass. He comes to establish a kingdom, and just when his immediate friends are thinking tremendous thoughts, that now at last he is about to set up that kingdom, he says, 'I am going away', and he leaves such a kingdom in the hands of fishers and tax-gatherers.

Norman N. G. Cope

When Jesus died and rose from the dead, he commanded his followers to go into all the world and preach the Gospel, but he also told them to remain in Jerusalem until they should receive the power from on high. He promised that 'another' would come so that they would not be bereft like orphans. As they waited in that upper room praying, suddenly tongues of fire descended upon them and they were moved by extraordinary experiences. They became new men. They received new power and new courage. They left that room with a new message to preach and new powers to heal.

Ronald Spivey

Here is a man who was born in an obscure village, the child of a peasant woman. He worked in a carpenter's shop until he was thirty, and then for three years he was an itinerant preacher. He had no credentials but himself. While still a young man, the tide of popular opinion turned against him. His friends, the twelve men who had learned so much from him and had promised him their enduring loyalty, ran away and left him. He went through the mockery of a trial; he was nailed upon a cross between two thieves; when he was dead, he was taken down and laid in a borrowed grave through the pity of a friend.

Yet I am well within the mark when I say that all the armies that ever marched, and all the parliaments that ever sat, and all the kings that ever reigned, put together, have not affected the lives of men and women upon this earth as has this one solitary life.

Anonymous

Human and Divine

Brian Thornton

'I am who I am'; so Exodus records Yahweh's response to Moses' request for some form of validation of his proposed mission to lead the people out of Egyptian bondage (Exodus 3:14).

But the suggestion that this is more accurately translated as 'I am what I will be' is, I find, helpful in coming to terms with the concept of Christ's divine and human natures, without having to accept that God suffers from some kind of theological schizophrenia.

I have to admit that I have never considered the concept of the threefold God very helpful to my own understanding. Modern mathematics, and indeed eastern orthodoxy, seem able to prove that three will go into one, but I find it less than helpful in trying to unscramble the inexplicable, preferring to concentrate on the oneness of the Godhead who is and will always be a profound and tantalising mystery.

I have no problem in believing that the ultimate power – who has the awesome ability to create physical matter simply by uttering it into existence – would have any problem in divesting himself of all that makes him holy and separate, to become like one of us, with all our limitations.

If the Son of God, Jesus, is not human in the sense that I am, then what is the point of him being my model? Oh yes, I appreciate the sinless aspect of his humanity, but that aside, (if one can dismiss it in such a manner) when I read the Scriptures I discern a man who experienced all the same gamut of human emotions as I do – happiness and anger, joy and sadness, elation and fatigue. These are all the things that my Lord and I share in common. Of course, his humanity was humanity at its best, human life as it should be. Mine, well that's an entirely different story, but it doesn't stop me, however often I fail, from trying to emulate his example.

Last year I had the supreme privilege of having lunch with Nelson Mandela. I spent two hours in the company of the person whom I consider to be the greatest example of someone who has lived his life on the pattern of Jesus. He would not claim to be perfect, but the generosity of spirit, the enthusiasm for the values that Jesus stood for, the infectiousness which has spread right throughout Southern Africa and created this most attractive rainbow people, is fashioned on the life that was lived by the God of history when he walked this earth almost two thousand years ago.

The meeting with the man who replaced retribution with reconciliation, who demanded honesty as a means of release from past wrongs, a person who might well have harboured all sorts of resentments and an 'I'll get my own back on you, just you wait and see' mentality, in reality mirrors the costly caring of his Lord.

Forty-eight hours before meeting the great man I had visited Robben Island, where he had spent eighteen of what should have been his most creative years incarcerated in a small 8ft x 6ft cell. I saw the quarry where he and others were made to break limestones into small pieces – those same stones worked on over the years are still there, as there was no purpose or use in this exercise. I asked myself how I would have reacted to such an experience, once given my freedom and the power and office to do anything I wanted?

For me, people like Nelson Mandela become a kind of bridge between the divine and human, so that perhaps instead of being total opposites, we can begin to see that they are but two sides of the same coin.

Scripture affirms that we are made in the image of our Creator, and the Christian rationale to explain the dichotomy of this is the fall from grace in the Garden, and the coining of the phrase 'original sin'. No doubt something quite horrific went wrong somewhere along the line, but what perhaps in part makes God divine is his refusal to ever stop believing in us, and the personal risks he is prepared to take to save us and to ensure a transformation to the original and good model.

For me, the sheer wonder of this holy God is that the power who can do and have anything he wants, wants nothing more than to have us experience the intimacy of a love affair with him. I don't begin to understand why, but I do assert with all my being that I know it to be a fact.

Now I am well aware that the words I have just used bring us dangerously near to a familiarity which is totally inappropriate when confronting this loving, but awesome and ultimately unknowable God. Sadly, I find too often the chummy approach of some Christian worship, born out of the belief in a kind of 'my mate Jesus' leaves no room whatsoever for the sheer wonder, adoration and reverend fear which surely must be our only appropriate stance when we approach the throne of grace. For undoubtedly, as someone once said, our arms are too short, our eyes too dim, our understanding virtually nil, when we, like Isaiah, are brought into the presence of the God of time and space. And yet, for me, worship, at its best, should be this kind of experience, a total giving of oneself to the sheer majesty and fear of this most demanding of all lovers.

In conclusion I come back to the problems I have with the doctrine of the Trinity, and apologise for being such a heretic in these matters, but the most helpful understanding of the kaleidoscopic nature of God is, for me, seen best on Calvary's Hill. I see there, not the man Jesus who utters in despair, 'It is finished' but a divine God who so desperately cares for that part of his creation made in his own image, that he is prepared to risk all, even his divinity, to prove just how far he is prepared to go to show us how much he is in love with us.

In one sense I see the cry 'It is finished' not as a human cry of defeat, but as a triumphant God (God who voluntarily reduced himself to human limitations) exclaiming as he witnesses to the indestructible power of that love, the culmination of his creative acts. For me, Good Friday in one sense is the seventh day of Creation. Far from resting, God engages in his finest work. At the centre of our faith there will always be, for me, this inexplicable mystery of how divinity became human, but until I am accorded, like St Paul, the opportunity to look into the mirror and see things clearly, I am content with the present baffling reflections of the inexplicable making sense.

When the Lord Jesus Christ returned to heaven he was met by the angel Gabriel who began to speak about the kingdom which Christ had founded.

'What arrangements have you made for your work to be carried on?' asked the angel.

'I have left eleven men,' replied Jesus.

'Are they rich, and influential, and clever?'

'No; they are mainly poor fishermen from the lakeside.'

'But are they capable speakers whose loyalty you have proved?'

'The leader of them, Simon Peter, has already denied three times that he knows me, and the others ran away when I was arrested,' Jesus replied.

'But, Lord,' exclaimed the angel, 'what if they fail you?'

'They will not fail,' said Jesus, 'I am counting on them.'

Anonymous

CONTRIBUTORS

Rev Canon David Adam is the Vicar of Holy Island off the Northumbrian coast. He is a poet and a keen photographer. The Island also provides the ideal environment for his other great love – the bird life. David Adam is deeply involved in teaching pilgrims, school groups and seekers about the Celtic vision of God, and of the all-pervading presence of the Trinity. Each year more than 140,000 people visit the Parish Church and a third of a million come to the Island. He says, 'This is a great opportunity for mission and outreach. It also lets us see how alive the church is throughout the nation – and how a great number of people are seekers.' David has written many books on prayer and meditation, mostly in the style of Celtic prayers. His books have been translated into twelve languages; they are used by Peruvian Christians in the Andes, Native Americans on a reservation, and by Christians beyond the Arctic Circle in Lapland. Above all, David believes we should talk *to* our God more than we talk *about* him.

Caro Ayres used to work for the Relief and Development Fund of the Methodist Church, (MRDF) but is now the Communications Officer for the Middle East, Europe and Central Asia team at Christian Aid. Brought up in Basingstoke, she worked in the West Bank and Gaza Strip after gaining a degree in Arabic. On her return to the UK, she completed an MA in Peace Studies, and then joined MRDF as Development Education Officer. Caro is an adventurous local preacher, an avid cinema-goer, shy piano player, and has recently discovered an interest in gardening.

Rt Rev John Austin Baker was born in 1928 and ordained to the Anglican ministry in 1955. He has served as parish priest, student chaplain, theology lecturer, Canon of Westminster, Chaplain to the Speaker of the House of Commons and diocesan bishop. Now retired, he and his wife Jill live in Winchester. John Austin Baker chaired the working party that produced *The Church and the Bomb* (1982) and bishops' groups that drafted *The Nature of Christian Belief* (1986) and *Issues in Human Sexuality* (1991). His publications include *The Foolishness of God* (1970), *Travels in Oudamovia* (1976), *The Whole Family of God* (1981) and *The Faith of a Christian* (1996). He was for several years involved in work for peace in Northern Ireland, and is active in the cause of animal welfare.

Deacon Sue Brecknell is a member of the Methodist Diaconal Order serving in the Bradford, Great Horton Circuit as a Community Development Worker, and also with the Methodist Touchstone Centre as Chaplain to the University of Bradford and Bradford College. Although born in the north-east, Sue lived in Nottinghamshire for 20 years, training on the East Midlands Ministerial Training Course in Nottingham, before taking up her first appointment in Bradford. She has been heavily involved in the field of HIV/AIDS, working directly with HIV-positive people. She writes liturgy and is very interested in group process, which informs her work, and ecclesiastical embroidery, which she undertakes in her spare time. Sue is influenced by liberation theology and is a part-time tutor at the Urban Theology Unit in Sheffield.

Wendy Craig was born in County Durham and trained as a teenager at London's Central School of Dramatic Art. She has appeared in numerous West End productions, including J. P. Donleavy's *The Ginger Man* with Richard Harris, David Mercer's *Ride a Cock Horse* with Peter O'Toole, and several stage revivals including *The Taming of the Shrew* and *Hobson's Choice*. Wendy Craig is perhaps best known for her television performances in the acclaimed *Butterflies* by Carla Lane, and the long-running drama series, *Nanny*, which was based on her own idea and format. In 1999 Wendy Craig appeared in Noel Coward's *Easy Virtue* at the Chichester Festival, and in 2000 she played Mrs Malaprop in *The Rivals* for the Royal Shakespeare Company. She has produced two cookery books – *Busy Mum's Cook Book* and *Busy Mum's Baking Book* – and edited a book of childhood memories of the famous, *Kid's Stuff*, for Save the Children Fund.

Rt Rev Ian Cundy has been Bishop of Peterborough since 1996. He was ordained in 1969 and served as an assistant curate in the Southwark diocese, taught church history and Christian doctrine at Oak Hill College, North London, and later became Team Rector of Mortlake with East Sheen. He was appointed Warden of Cranmer Hall Theological College, Durham in 1983 and was consecrated Area Bishop of Lewes in 1992.

Rev Dr Peter Graves is minister of Wesley Methodist Church, Cambridge, and Chaplain to Methodist students at the University. He is internationally known for his preaching and teaching ministry. Dr Graves has served some of the largest churches in Methodism and until recently was Superintendent minister of Central Hall, Westminster. He is a Vice-President of the Bible Society, writes daily Bible reading notes for the Bible Reading Fellowship, and is deeply committed to furthering the use of the Bible in the local church setting. He is a regular broadcaster, and has also published numerous articles in books and magazines.

Rev Donald Hilton is a minister of the United Reformed Church, having been ordained within Congregationalism. He ministered in three local churches: South Norwood, Gosport, and for sixteen years at Princes Street, Norwich. He was Christian Education Secretary of the Congregational Church in the period which saw the birth of *Partners in Learning*, and was Moderator of the Yorkshire Province of the URC for the final ten years of his ministry. He served as Moderator of the General Assembly of the URC in 1993-4. He has compiled five anthologies of worship material, and three books of prayers published by the NCEC. His *Table Talk*, published by the URC, is a radical reflection on the Communion Service. Having retired in 1997, he is currently a member of the United Reformed/Methodist Church in Bungay on the border of Norfolk and Suffolk.

Susan Howdle spent her schooldays in Yorkshire, where she met her future husband Peter, who is now a consultant physician at St James Hospital, Leeds and a Professor at Leeds Medical School. After studying Law at Lady Margaret Hall, Oxford, Susan was called to the Bar and then lectured in law for over twenty years at the Universities of Bristol and Sheffield. More recently her professional work has been in chairing Tribunals, and in 1998 she was appointed by the Lord Chancellor to the Council on Tribunals. Susan is a local preacher and pastoral visitor in the Leeds North East Circuit. She has served on a number of Methodist connexional committees, and is the Journal Secretary of the Methodist Conference. In 1993-4 she was Vice-President of the Conference, and since 1996 she has been Chair of Methodist Homes for the Aged. She and her husband have written about their experience of childlessness in the *Thorns in the Flesh* series, published by Methodist Publishing House (1993).

Rev Julie M. Hulme is a writer in the field of spirituality, who is following a call to live the Ministry of Word and Sacrament as a life of prayer. She is married to David, who is the Superintendent minister of the Birmingham (Elmdon) circuit, and they have two teenage daughters.

Dr Daleep Mukarji trained as a medical doctor and began his career working in a leprosy hospital in Dichapli, Andhra Pradesh in India, before moving to Medak, where he ran a 125-bed mission hospital. Becoming interested in public health issues in India, he established a rural health and community development programme at the Christian Medical College in Vellore, and in 1985 was appointed General Secretary of the Christian Medical Association of India, the health agency of the National Christian Council of Churches in India. By coincidence, both the rural health programme and the Christian Medical Association were funded by Christian Aid. At the same time, he became involved within ecumenical organisations, such as the Christian Conference of Asia. In 1994 he took up the post of Executive Secretary for Health, Community and Justice at the World Council of Churches in Geneva. His post as Director of Christian Aid began in April 1998.

Rev David Parkes studied engineering at Manchester University and completed his engineering training with Rolls-Royce. He spent fifteen years in bio-engineering and management roles with the Department of Health, involved primarily with users, health professionals, research establishments and manufacturers in the supply of rehabilitation equipment. David then trained for the presbyteral ministry at Wesley College in Bristol. In both his Methodist circuit appointments he also served as a prison chaplain, and he is currently a chaplain to the hospitals in Peterborough.

Prue Phillipson was brought up in Newcastle upon Tyne, gained a BA in English at London University and trained as a teacher. She married and had five children, and during their school years she wrote articles and short stories, winning several prizes. She also did some supply teaching and adult evening classes. Through a Council of Churches Study Group on Law and Order she became involved in voluntary work with offenders on Community Service and later was appointed a Sessional Supervisor. She later gave this up to care for her elderly mother, and an account of these years has been published as *Lesson of Love* (Foundery Press). She has also published two novels set in Hexham where she and her husband have lived since 1974, and these with two more novels and a volume of short stories are to be published on the Internet. Her Christian faith inspires her fiction and non-fiction work alike.

Rev Ray Simpson spent some time working for the Bible Society, after which he planted The Christian Church in Bowthorpe, Norwich, sponsored by six denominations. He was both Vicar and Methodist minister. He also founded Bowthorpe Community Trust, which enabled a Work and Worship area to develop at the heart of this new neighbourhood. In 1994 he was appointed Hon. Guardian of the ecumenical network of Christians, The Community of Aidan and Hilda, and two years later he moved to Lindisfarne, where the Community now has its office and Retreat House, *The Open Gate*. Here he nurtures a cradling of Christian spirituality inspired by Celtic saints, through retreats, consultations with church leaders, soul friendship, church workshops and writing of study and devotional resources. He is the author of *Give Yourself A Retreat* and of other books published by Hodder & Stoughton, which include *Exploring Celtic Spirituality: Historic Roots for our Future, Celtic Worship through the Year, Celtic Daily Light* and *Celtic Blessings for Everyday*. His latest book is *Soul Friendship: Celtic Insights Into Spiritual Mentoring*.

Rev Phil Summers is a Methodist minister in the Wolverhampton (Trinity) circuit, with a responsibility for Drama, the Connexional Team.

Rt Rev James Thompson was educated at Emmanuel College, Cambridge and Cuddesdon Theological College. He was appointed a curate in East Ham in 1966, and served in a number of appointments, becoming Bishop of Stepney in 1978, and Bishop of Bath and Wells in 1991. Among a large number of appointments, he has served as Co-Chairman of the Inter-Faith Network from 1987-92, and as Chairman of the British Council of Churches Committee for Relations with People of Other Faiths from 1983-90. A member of the General Synod of the Church of England, he is also a regular broadcaster on television and radio, especially BBC Radio 4. His publications include *The Lord's Song* (Fontana 1990), *Stepney Calling* (Cassell 1991) and *Why God? Thinking Through Faith* (Cassell 1996).

Brian Thornton, a Yorkshire man, is Chief Executive of the Methodist Publishing House. A local preacher, he is Trustee of Wesley House, Cambridge, and Secretary of the International Publishing Committee of the World Methodist Council. He was Vice-President of the Methodist Conference 1999-2000. He believes that Methodism both has a future and is called upon to make a distinctive contribution to that longed-for treasure house of faith – a united church in England. He longs for the day when the church can, in unison, proclaim the good news of Jesus Christ. He and his wife Brenda (a retired teacher) have revelled, during the last two years, in their new status of grandparents – three times over!

Rev Gordon Wakefield has been a Methodist minister for almost sixty years. As well as Circuit ministry he has been Connexional Editor, Chairman of the Manchester and

Stockport District and Principal of the Ecumenical Queens College, Birmingham. He has taught and written on Liturgy and Spirituality. He was the first Methodist to be awarded a Lambeth DD.

Doreen Warman is a Methodist who has led both Junior church and a Brownie pack. In her career as a social worker and later at the Citizens' Advice Bureau she has enjoyed working with people from all walks of life. She loves contemporary versions of the New Testament which give its message fresh impact and relevance for today's world. Doreen is the author of *It's Just a Thought* (Foundery Press) – a collection of ideas about God in everyday life.

Flora Slosson Wuellner is a minister in the United Church of Christ (Congregational branch) in the United States. After some years in parish ministry, she moved into a specialised ministry of spiritual renewal which has included retreat leadership, spiritual direction, and thirteen years as adjunct faculty member at the Pacific School of Religion in Berkeley, California. She has written a number of books on the relationship of spiritual renewal to the health of our personalities. Several of her books have been published in the UK by Eagle Press.

ACKNOWLEDGEMENTS

Methodist Publishing House gratefully acknowledges the use of copyright items. Every effort has been made to trace copyright owners, but where we have been unsuccessful we would welcome information which would enable us to make appropriate acknowledgement in any reprint.

Scripture quotations, unless otherwise stated, are from the New Revised Standard Version of the Bible, copyright 1989 by the Division of Christian Education of the National Council of the Churches of Christ in the USA.

Page

8   Caryll Houselander, 'She is a reed', Sheed & Ward Ltd. Permission applied for.

10   David Rhymer, *Glimpses in Faith*, Bishop of Truro's Lis. Escop. Gp., edited Stephen Dawes.

11   Carmina Gadelica, collected by Alexander Carmichael (as arranged by C. J. Moore for Floris Books, 1994). By permission of Floris Books.

'For nine months', Tadg Gaelach O Suillegbhain, *A Celtic Miscellany*, K. H. Jackson (trans.), Penguin Classics, 1971. Permission applied for.

12   'Babe of Heaven', Ray Simpson, *Celtic Daily Light*, Hodder & Stoughton, 1998. Permission applied for.

14   Extract from 'The Dream of the Rood', ed. and trans. Kevin Crossley-Holland, *The Anglo-Saxon World*, Blydell and Brewer Ltd. Permission applied for.

15   'O Son of God', Irish, Tadhg Og O Huiginn, *A Celtic Miscellany*, K. H. Jackson (trans.), Penguin Classics, 1971. Permission applied for.

20   Eric Milner-White, *My God, My Glory*, reproduced by kind permission of The Friends of York Minster.

26   Eleanor Farjeon, 'The Old Shepherds', Faber & Faber Limited. Permission applied for.

27   © George Appleton, *The Quiet Heart*, Fount 1983. Permission applied for.

29   Thomas Baird, 'The Message of Advent', *Preacher's Handbook 2*, Epworth Press.

35   Carlo Carretto, *Letters from the Desert*, Orbis Books, 1972.

44   William Barclay, *The Gospel of Mark*, The Daily Study Bible, Saint Andrew Press.

52   Alex Findlay, 'Glimpses from the life of Jesus', *Preacher's Handbook 7*, Epworth Press.

54   Mary Evelyn Jegen, SND, *How You Can Be A Peacemaker*, by permission of the author.

59   Brian Jenner, 'From the Circuits', *Epworth Review* September 1984.

61   Bryan Rippin, *The Christian Juggler*, Epworth Press.

62   Joan Puls, *Every Bush is Burning*, WCC Publications, Geneva.

62   Michael Palmer, *Glimpses in Faith*, Bishop of Truro's Lis. Escop. Gp., edited Stephen Dawes.

62   C. Edgar Wilkinson, *The Comings of Christ,* Epworth Press.

68   John Carmody, *The Heart of the Christian Matter,* Abingdon Press.

92   Maurice Friggens, *Glimpses in Faith,* Bishop of Truro's Lis. Escop. Gp., edited Stephen Dawes.

93   Lloyd John Ogilvie, *Radiance of the Inner Splendour,* Permission applied for.

95   Stephen Neill, *A Genuinely Human Existence,* Doubleday, a division of Random House Inc.

100   David Francis, 'Not Yet', *Epworth Review,* May 1985.

101   Bruce Barton, *The Book Nobody Knows,* Constable.

101   Francis Brienen, 1994, from *A Restless Hope,* the Prayer Handbook for 1995, published by the United Reformed Church.

102   Albert Frederick Bayly, 'Lord, whose love through humble service', Words by Albert F. Bayly (1901-84) © 1988 Oxford University Press. Reproduced by permission.

108   Georgia Harkness, 'Hope of the world'. Words copyright © 1954. Renewal 1982 by the Hymn Society/Hope Publishing Co. Administered by CopyCare, PO Box 77, Hailsham, BN27 3EF, UK. Music@copycare.com> Used by permission.

110   Robert V. Dodd, *Praying the Name of Jesus,* copyright © 1985 by The Upper Room. Used by permission of Upper Room Books.

111 John Williams, *Glimpses in Faith*, Bishop of Truro's Lis. Escop. Gp., edited Stephen Dawes.

118 Wendy M. Wright, 'Lord, when did we see you?', *Weavings* (Mar/April 1990). Used by permission of The Upper Room.

134 David Deeks, 'Church building: a way of doing theology', *Epworth Review*, May 1984.

141 Martin Eggleton, *Pain-Bearers*, Methodist Publishing House.

150 Gerald Vann, *The High Green Hill*, Collins. Permission applied for.

152 Stephen Dawes, *Glimpses in Faith*, Bishop of Truro's Lis. Escop. Gp., edited Stephen Dawes.

153 James Asa Johnson, 'It must have happened in later years', Faber & Faber Limited. Permission applied for.